# Florida and World War II

## A Personal Recollection

*Jim Wiggins*

HERITAGE BOOKS
2008

# HERITAGE BOOKS
*AN IMPRINT OF HERITAGE BOOKS, INC.*

### Books, CDs, and more—Worldwide

For our listing of thousands of titles see our website
at
www.HeritageBooks.com

Published 2008 by
HERITAGE BOOKS, INC.
Publishing Division
100 Railroad Ave. #104
Westminster, Maryland 21157

Copyright © 2008 Jim Wiggins

All rights reserved. No part of this book may be reproduced or transmitted in any form or by any means, electronic or mechanical, including photocopying, recording or by any information storage and retrieval system without written permission from the author, except for the inclusion of brief quotations in a review.

International Standard Book Number: 978-0-7884-4545-3

# Dedication

This book is dedicated to the young men and women of Florida who sacrificed their lives for the sake of freedom in a war that was thrust upon them. The list includes the older boy next door, the uncle down the street, the cousin who taught you how to throw a football, and the countless numbers of strangers who readily accepted the call for sacrifice.

# Table of Contents

|  | Page |
|---|---|
| Dedication | iii |
| Table of Contents | v |
| List of Illustrations | vii |
| Acknowledgements | xi |
| Introduction | xiii |
| **Chapter One** | 1 |
|     The Growing Signs of War | |
| **Chapter Two** | 19 |
|     War is Declared | |
| **Chapter Three** | 25 |
|     Florida's Military Bases | |
| **Chapter Four** | 61 |
|     The War on Florida's East Coast | |
| **Chapter Five** | 81 |
|     U-Boats in the Gulf | |
| **Chapter Six** | 95 |
|     Germans on Florida Soil | |
| **Chapter Seven** | 109 |
|     Florida's Economic Expansion | |
| **Chapter Eight** | 119 |
|     The Home Front | |
| **Chapter Nine** | 153 |
|     They Remember | |
| Notes | 177 |
| BIBLIOGRAPHY | 183 |
| INDEX | 187 |

# List of Illustrations

| Illustration | Page |
|---|---|
| Photo 1 – FDR tried to convince the US Congress with Fireside Chats to amend the Neutrality Act. This cartoon by George White was published in October 1941 and depicts Europe under siege by the Germans while the debate continued. *(Florida Archives)* | 8 |
| Photo 2 – Headlines in newspapers across Florida screamed the news of the Pearl Harbor Attack on December 7, 1941. This headline in the *Tallahassee News-Democrat* was a special edition. *(Florida Archives)* | 21 |
| Photo 3 – Crowds filled a school in Leon County in 1940 when registration for Selective Service began. Men between the ages of 21 to 36 were required to sign up for the Draft. *(Florida Archives)* | 24 |
| Photo 4 – British cadets and their instructors pose outside their aircraft at Carlstrom Field in 1940 at Arcadia. *(Florida Archives)* | 27 |
| Photo 5 – British Royal Navy pilots arrive for training in 1940 at the Pensacola Naval Air Station. *(Florida Archives)* | 29 |
| Photo 6 – This aerial view of a portion of Camp Blanding includes the hospital complex. *(Florida Archives)* | 33 |
| Photo 7 – Men from Company M, 124th Infantry, join in maneuvers at Camp Blanding. *(Florida Archives)* | 34 |
| Photo 8 – A parade and review is held at the Dale Mabry Air Field in Tallahassee. *(Florida Archives)* | 37 |
| Photo 9 – Florida National Guardsmen participate in maneuvers at National Bridge in Leon County. *(Florida Archives)* | 38 |
| Photo 10 – Men wait in the chow line at Camp Gordon Johnson in 1943. *(Florida Archives)* | 39 |
| Photo 11 – This memorial stands in Arcadia to honor 23 British RAF cadets who lost their lives while training in Florida. *(Florida Archives)* | 42 |
| Photo 12 – P-51D Mustangs wait for takeoff at MacDill Army Air Base in Tampa for joint American, British, and French aerial training and operations. *(Florida Archives)* | 43 |
| Photo 13 – Navy pilots pose at Fort Lauderdale Naval Air Station, July 1943. President George H.W. Bush, who learned to fly Grumman TBF Avenger torpedo bombers, is standing in the back row, second from right. *(NAS Fort Lauderdale H.A. Museum)* | 45 |
| Photo 14 – Army Air Corp soldiers receive training on the white sands of Miami Beach. *(Florida Archives)* | 47 |
| Photo 15 – US Navy dive-bombers fly over the city of Miami. *(Florida Archives)* | 48 |
| Photo 16 – Lookout towers like this one on Hutchinson Island were distributed all along the Atlantic and Gulf coastlines to watch for German submarines or enemy aircraft. *(Florida Archives)* | 69 |
| Photo 17 – A tanker is ablaze off Jupiter Inlet after being hit by a German submarine. *(Florida Archives)* | 73 |

| Illustration | Page |
|---|---|
| Photo 18 – The tanker, *Gulfland*, burns a short distance off Hobe Sound after being torpedoed by a German submarine. *(Florida Archives)* | 75 |
| Photo 19 – A shrimp boat moves close to rescue survivors from a sinking freighter in the Gulf of Mexico. *(Florida Archives)* | 88 |
| Photo 20 – This map shows the location of ships sunk in 1942 by German submarines. *(Historical Museum of Southern Florida)* | 92 |
| Photo 21 – German POWs learn English in a classroom at Camp Blanding. *(Florida Archives)* | 102 |
| Photo 22 – German POWs pick oranges in central Florida. *(US National Archives)* | 104 |
| Photo 23 – The Tampa Shipyards grew quickly until they were employing 20,000 workers. *(Florida Archives)* | 111 |
| Photo 24 – Wooden ships are being built at the Oscar Daniels Shipyard in Tampa. *(Florida Archives)* | 117 |
| Photo 25 – Shown here is the draft card of Roy Estes of Miami, which is typical of those issued by local selective service boards. *(Florida Archives)* | 121 |
| Photo 26 – Mr. And Mrs. William H. Neff and their son, Morris, appear before a grand jury on charges that Morris was hidden for three years in his home to avoid the draft. *(Florida Archives)* | 123 |
| Photo 27 – The first stamps for gasoline rationing were issued on December 1, 1942. *(Florida Archives)* | 126 |
| Photo 28 – Gov. Spessard L. Holland views defense posters in 1943. *(Florida Archives)* | 127 |
| Photo 29 – Defense posters reminded citizens to buy US savings stamps and bonds. *(Florida Archives)* | 131 |
| Photo 30 – Volunteers sign up at the Civic Exhibition Center in St. Petersburg. *(Florida Archives)* | 132 |
| Photo 31 – Residents of Leesburg proudly display their large pile of scrap metal collected for the war cause. *(Florida Archives)* | 133 |
| Photo 32 – Children proudly display their collection of pots and pans for a scrap metal drive outside the Roxy Theatre in Tampa. *(Florida Archives)* | 134 |
| Photo 33 – Students at Florida State College tend their victory garden. *(Florida Archives)* | 135 |
| Photo 34 – Students and faculty form a "V for Victory" on the campus of the Florida State College in Tallahassee. *(Florida Archives)* | 136 |
| Photo 35 – Sniff Kits were distributed throughout Florida schools by the US Army to make students aware of possible enemy threats with the use of chemical warfare. *(Florida Archives)* | 144 |
| Photo 36 – Truck convoys traveled regularly on Florida highways. This convoy from Camp Blanding was waiting to load soldiers. *(Florida Archives)* | 146 |
| Photo 37 – Servicemen gather at the USO in Jacksonville. *(Florida Archives)* | 148 |
| Photo 38 – USO activities for servicemen at Tallahassee included dances and outings. *(Florida Archives)* | 149 |
| Photo 39 – Telegram from War Department. *(Jewel Hardin)* | 153 |

| Illustration | Page |
|---|---|
| Photo 40 – Milton Earl Hardin of Ellenton, Florida, was reported missing in action before his daring escape from a German prison camp. *(Jewel Hardin)* | 154 |
| Photo 41 – Captain Colin P. Kelly, Jr., of Madison, Florida, was credited with being the first US war hero. *(Florida Archives)* | 170 |
| Photo 42 – "Ace of Aces" Capt. David McCampbell of West Palm Beach set a record in aerial warfare history during World War II. *(Florida Archives.)* | 172 |
| Photo 43 – Servicemen read the news about the Japanese surrender in the *St. Petersburg Times*. *(Florida Archives)* | 173 |
| Photo 44 – Sailors climb the light posts in Miami to celebrate the end of war. *(Florida Archives)* | 174 |
| Photo 45 – Headlines from Jacksonville's *Florida Times-Union* proclaims hope for a world of peace. *(Florida Archives)* | 175 |

# Acknowledgements

Again, I wish to acknowledge the sacrifices made by those who served their country so valiantly during World War 11, including the loved ones who remained at home and waited anxiously for their return. I am indebted to friends and relatives such as Gloria Condo and Donna Simpson who shared their experiences and to the countless numbers who offered their memories.

Photos are an essential part of this endeavor and I am appreciative for the assistance offered by such persons as Adam Watson of the Florida Archives and staff members of *The Tampa Tribune, The St. Petersburg Times,* NAS Historical Association Museum of Ft. Lauderdale, The Historical Museum of Southern Florida, and The National Archives.

I am indebted to Jewel Hardin, wife of Earl Hardin, who graciously shared the material for the last chapter and I am especially indebted to Barbara Casey, literary agent, who is responsible for the sizeable job of getting this material ready to meet the specifications required by Heritage Books, Inc. The project has reached fruition because of her dedicated effort and I am eternally grateful. Lastly, I thank my wife, Colleen, for her patience and understanding as I spend hours upon hours in front of the word processor with one project after another.

Jim Wiggins
# Introduction

During my childhood while growing up at Ellenton, Florida, I heard many war stories from my uncle, Harry Condo, who lived next door and was a pilot during World War I. He was one among forty-two thousand Floridians who served in a war optimistically and erroneously referred to by President Woodrow Wilson as "the war to end all wars." The tragic war years of 1914-18 claimed more than 10 million lives and it was assumed that a tragedy of such momentous proportions could never be repeated, a rather naive notion. Less than two decades later there was an ill wind blowing once again that would stir up animosities leading to another worldwide involvement that would reach into the far corners of the world, including every little staid community of Florida, which was called home.

Florida would hold a unique position in that conflict, an involvement that went far beyond the enrollment of 250,000 young men in the Armed Services. The Sunshine State was more totally immersed in World War II than any other state, not only because of its precarious geographical location as a peninsula between the Gulf and the Atlantic Ocean with seaports to facilitate shipping, but also because of ideal climate and flat land that would serve well as bases for military personnel. Indeed, the Sunshine State would be called upon to play a highly significant role unlike any other in the United States.

Living in Florida during that time was unique for those of us who were sandwiched between the years of the Great Depression and World War II. It is from this perspective that I write this account of a period between 1941 and 1945, an era into which we were thrust by circumstances beyond our control. To view history from within such a context will, conceivably, offer readers a greater chance to more fully understand and appreciate

## Jim Wiggins

the extreme complexities of those years when Florida's history was being radically changed. Admittedly, a bit of what I write about is *perceived* history because of my involvement from a personal perspective. Hopefully, it will help facilitate readers' interest and complement the factual accounts about the real stuff, which I have included after several years of research, information which is available to anyone who is willing to search out facts about what was going on in Florida during those critical years when our nation was united in a common cause. World War II provided an adhesive unity like none other in US history. Ours was a united front, unlike that experienced by the citizenry during the years of the Vietnam War, the Korean War, or the misguided involvement in Iraq. True, most people initially supported isolationism and many questioned FDR's decision to support our overseas allies prior to the war but few questioned whether the cause was just or not after the attack on Pearl Harbor. War was declared; everyone rallied around the flag, and Floridians were right in the middle of it.

# Chapter One

# The Growing Signs of War

It soon became obvious that the first worldwide war involving nearly thirty nations was not the ultimate solution to the world's problems and was not sufficient to ward off the rising tension created by such nations as Germany, Italy and Japan. The rise of Adolph Hitler's leadership in the early 1930s and Mussolini's invasion of Ethiopia in 1935 gave concern for all democracies while Japan coiled like a snake ready to strike out with its deadly venom. Public opinion in the United States, however, was overwhelmingly supportive of neutrality, prompting such men as Senator Harry S. Truman to implore leadership to simply allow the dictators "to fight it out."[1] His remarks followed Germany's invasion of the Soviet Union and expressed the common sentiment felt by US citizens.

On the other hand, President Franklin D. Roosevelt emphatically rebuked the tendency toward isolationism at a time when allied nations were facing possible annihilation by Germans seeking worldwide dominance. Despite the majority of negative public opinion that had been conditioned, in part, by the suffering wrought during the Great Depression, the president was privately determined to support nations such as France and Britain in their struggle against their oppressors who were becoming increasingly overt in their operations.

President Roosevelt's hands were tied by the leadership in Washington and by an apprehensive public, including Floridians, who were witnessing economic growth and security that had been unknown for so many years. Struggling working-class families were welcoming a new era and the future looked bright. No one was inclined to give that up. Roosevelt was frustrated in his inability to educate his people about what was happening in the world and how that would have a negative effect on American security. Hitler's terrorizing destruction in Poland and his rampage in Europe readily ignited the wrath of the world and Roosevelt felt more strongly that neutrality simply could not be an option for the United States. He finally determined that some move was necessary so in September of 1939 the president set up a neutrality zone patrol of US warships, designed to avoid any warlike activity in close waters offshore of North and South America. The naval patrol was ordered to report the presence of any enemy submarines or any suspicious vessels in the area. Germany was not upset with this arrangement since they assumed that their submarines could continue traveling regularly along the shoreline between North and South America with immunity. They had become quite glib in accepting the US control of all movements in the region. However, they soon realized that the reports from naval patrols about all ships were to be in English only. This practice was helpful to British warships that could pick up messages about German targets in the area.

A bit of the president's frustration was greatly relieved when, in late 1939, he was able to vent his anger in an incident that took place on Florida's southeast coast. It was in that year that Florida was to have its first major role in the struggle that would inevitably lead to World War II.

On December 19, 1939, a new diesel powered German freighter, the *Aruca*, was returning from a trip to Brazil and, after being reported by a US patrol, was intercepted by the British cruiser, the *Orion*. The German freighter was forced to take refuge in Port Everglades to escape fire from the cruiser. A German ship anchored in Florida brought quite a stir to Southeast residents and curious Fort Lauderdale citizens turned out in droves to view the ship and its uninvited visitors. One English gentleman, A.H. Brook, who called himself a *Commodore*, extended hospitality to the crew by delivering food, magazines and other items to make them comfortable. A local newsman, Holt McPherson, even claimed that the man provided detailed maps of the port's waters.

"Then all hell broke loose," McPherson wrote, when the US State Department stated that people were violating the neutrality agreement of the government. "Hell, we ain't neutral," responded Brook.[4] Cases of beer were delivered to the ship by friendly citizens and Frederick Stengler was even invited aboard the ship for a Christmas party. He reported that the captain was "bouncy" and "enthusiastic," elated over his narrow escape and bragged that the war would be over before his return to Germany. He also bragged that his "cover," the battleship *Graf Spee*, would soon destroy the *Orion,* which was still waiting offshore. However, he soon learned that his "cover" had already been blown up by the British in the waters off Montevideo in Uruguay and that the captain had committed suicide.[5]

Florida's role in this intriguing incident got even more interesting when the president of the United States paid a visit. The freighter remained in the port for the entire year of 1940 and was watched closely by the Coast Guard and immigration officials. Then, in late March 1941, President Roosevelt and his friend, Harry Hopkins, were returning from a fishing trip off the Florida coast and the president became aware of the freighter sitting in port with a Nazi flag waving overhead. He was infuriated and asked for information about its presence. On March 30, before returning by train to Washington, the president ordered that the freighter be seized and that the cocky Captain Steinger and the crew of 52 men be incarcerated. He also ordered that any other Nazi vessels within American ports be seized. Fifty-three others throughout the US were immediately boarded and taken over by the Coast Guard. (The *Aruca* was later used to haul shipments of nitrate between the United States and South America.)

Many criticized President Roosevelt for the action taken in Florida while Congress and the majority of US citizens still supported the Neutrality Act. However, the president took great delight in being able to circumvent laws in a cause, which he deemed to be right. FDR's biographer and speech writer Robert Sherwood, director of the Office of War Information, later wrote that no single episode of those dark and perilous early years had given the president more sheer pleasure than what took place at Port Everglades.[6] (His book, *Roosevelt and Hopkins* received the 1948 Pulitzer prize.) Congress was slowly beginning to realize that the United States could no longer ignore the monstrous acts of Hitler that encroached on the world and threatened security for American citizens.

FDR and Winston Churchill of Britain held similar views of Hitler's reckless siege for power but Roosevelt, unfortunately, was compelled to restrain his feelings. Jon Meacham in his recent book, *Franklin and Winston, an Intimate Portrait of an Epic Friendship*, offered a thorough analysis of the common bond of the two. He emphasized that, despite their common cause, only Churchill was able to speak his mind openly in public in the early years because of the wariness of the American citizens to assist the

British people in their plight. Roosevelt, however, offered his personal support to Churchill in the early days of war and admired his will to fight what appeared to be a losing war at times.[3]

After many months of restraint, the president went public on June 10, 1940, in Charlottesville, Virginia. He proclaimed that the United States could not remain a "lone island in a world dominated by the philosophy of force."[7] He immediately took steps to assist allies in their struggle, including a move within months to supply Britain with 50 destroyers requested by Winston Churchill in their fight against German U-boats. In return, the British gave 99-year leases for US naval and air bases on British possessions such as Newfoundland and Jamaica.

Roosevelt defended his move as an act of exchange that benefited both parties. It was obvious that this step would move the US closer to war. His resolve to prepare the nation for war was further strengthened by the passage of the Selective Service Act. The draft, of course, greatly involved the personal lives of American citizens and no family would be exempt from the conscription of their loved ones and friends by their government.

Roosevelt and his presidential opponent during the 1940 election, Wendell Wilkie, both declared their intentions to keep the US out of the war. As part of the political strategy to win the election, both men supported plans to send economic help to democracies in their struggle against their enemies. Roosevelt's third election in November assured him that the public supported his positions of involvement by the United States in the world struggle. Congress immediately passed a land-lease bill of seven billion dollars that would assist allied nations, an act that Washington's leadership finally conceded to be vital for American security.

Families sat glued to their radios during those eventful years to listen to the latest news about world events. My parents, for example, would settle down by the radio to listen to FDR's fireside chats, which usually lasted about six to ten minutes. On a 9:30 p.m. message in May 1940 the president expressed his growing concern and frustration at dealing with the increasing hostility of Germany as Hitler's bombers wrought havoc over France and Belgium. He extended his talk and begged his listeners to give generously to the Red Cross, which was "rushing food and clothing and medical supplies to the destitute civilian millions." He expressed concern that many Americans felt that the war "was none of our business; that no matter what happened over there, the United States could always pursue its peaceful and unique course in the world."[8] He continued in his attempt to change public opinion:

*There are many among us who closed their eyes, from lack of interest or lack of knowledge, honestly and sincerely thinking that the many hundreds of miles and salt water made the American Hemisphere so remote that the people of the North and Central and South America could go on living in the midst of their vast resources without reference to, or danger from, other Continents of the world.*

*There are some among us who were persuaded by minority groups that we could maintain our physical safety by retiring within our continental boundaries...the Atlantic on the east, the Pacific on the west, Canada on the north and Mexico on the south. I illustrated the futility...the impossibility...of that idea in my Message to the Congress last week. Obviously, a defense policy based on that is merely to invite future attack.*

*And, finally, there are a few among us who have deliberately and consciously closed their eyes because they were determined to be opposed to their government, its foreign policy and every other policy, to be partisan, and to believe that anything that the Government did was wholly wrong.*[9]

The president stressed the futility of isolationism and US

tendencies to retreat from its responsibilities. He also discussed charges that Americans were not prepared for war. He pointed out how the US had spent large sums of money on national defense, used in part "to make our Army and Navy today the largest, the best equipped, and the best trained peace-time military establishment in the whole history of this country."[10]

The president recognized that there was a lot of fear that bordered on panic but stressed that the country should feel secure in its ability to meet the challenges. He explained how much money had been spent to upgrade the military after he took office in 1933 and detailed the current strength of the military, emphasizing the need to upgrade and reappraise the country's production rate, stating at the same time that he would authorize money to be spent.

There was no doubt that the president was insisting that the people of the US be ready for the inevitable war. They could no longer be isolationists. He continued:

> *Yes, we are calling upon the resources, the efficiency and the ingenuity of the American manufacturers of war material of all kinds...airplanes and tanks and guns and ships, and all the hundreds of products that go into this material. The Government of the United States itself manufactures few of the implements of war. Private industry will continue to be the source of most of this material, and private industry will have to be speeded up to produce it at the rate and efficiency called for by the needs of the time. Therefore, the Government of the United States stands ready to advance the necessary money to help provide for the enlargement of factories, the establishment of new plants, the employment of thousands of necessary workers, the development of new sources of supply for the hundreds of raw*

materials required, the development of quick mass transportation of supplies. And the details of all of this are being worked out in Washington day and night.[11]

The president stated emphatically that haste in preparing for war should in no way have a negative impact upon social values or employment standards. He also stressed continued concern for the poor and stated that "no new group of war

Photo 1. FDR tried to convince the US Congress with Fireside Chats to amend the Neutrality Act. This cartoon by George White was published in October, 1941 and depicts Europe under siege by the Germans while the debate continued. *(Florida Archives)*

millionaires shall come into being in this nation as a result of the struggles abroad. The American people will not relish the idea of any American citizen growing rich and fat in an emergence of blood and slaughter and human suffering."[12] Indeed, there were

## Jim Wiggins

few areas of concern that the president overlooked in his unusually long and detailed address on this Sunday evening of May 26. He emphasized that the United States would be capable of meeting the forces of destruction and sought to reassure those who were pessimistic about the future. He stressed the importance of support for a free society and urged the American people to continue in their resolve with a human spirit of will and determination to continue building upon the democratic principles established by the founding fathers.

His closing remarks called for the prayers of the people with a plea, "that all of us beg that suffering and starving, that death and destruction may end and that peace may return to the world."[13]

But FDR knew that he was still treading on the edge and had to move cautiously, doing so while ensuring solidarity with Great Britain without having the approval of Congress. During the last six months of 1941, FDR led the United States into virtual co-belligerency with Great Britain in the battle of the Atlantic. He did so in stages, often using incidents resulting from one action to gain support for the next. American naval vessels had for some time been tracking U-boats and radioing their whereabouts to the British. In July, the United States occupied Iceland and began convoying merchant vessels to adjacent waters. When a German submarine fired two torpedoes at the American destroyer *Greer* in September, Roosevelt used this as a pretext to announce a "shoot on sight" policy. (He neglected to mention that the *Greer* had been tailing the U-boat for several hours.) He similarly manipulated American opinion following the attack on the destroyer *Kearny* and the sinking of the *Reuben James* in October. In the next month, he succeeded in having Congress remove virtually all restrictions on American shipping. His critics protested in vain.

Martin Gilbert, in his book *The Second World War*, devotes a chapter on the climate of the times in 1940 with emphasis on FDR's insistence that the world was facing "a new order of tyranny." He stressed that allied friends could not afford to sit idly by without giving assistance. The period between January and March 1941, was described as "the widening war" while the intensity of Hitler's strikes increased. Roosevelt's diplomatic skills helped tremendously to change the minds of many who were still in denial.[14]

And you'd better believe that people everywhere, including those in Florida, could no longer help but notice what was taking place. True, the general public knew little about world geography and were quite confused about differing ideologies, but the climate of complacency was being threatened by the reality of war and it was rapidly becoming apparent that democratic nations could not simply put their heads in the sand and pretend that all was right with the world. The media, influenced greatly by the president's passionate fireside chats, was encroaching on the consciences of American citizens, including Floridians, who were increasingly being bombarded with propaganda to support our allies across the ocean. Obviously, the subject of approaching war was of paramount concern throughout the United States.

There seemed to be a cloud hanging over us during those years of 1940-41 and no one knew what lay in store for those of us privileged to live in Florida. Our preachers admonished God for help and our favorite radio shows were interrupted with news about casualties in Europe. We watched the newsreels that were shown while attending the "picture shows" on Saturday afternoons at the theater in Bradenton. We saw soldiers from other countries at war and witnessed bombs falling. But I must admit that as a naive 11-year-old I never fully comprehended that all of that fighting on the world scene might somehow have something to do with me or my friends. We were much more interested in discovering whether Flash Gordon would survive his crash or whether Tarzan would be able to rescue Jane from the cliff where she was hanging the Saturday before. The reality of war and death had simply not struck home, despite the newsreels, which showed bombs falling on London and elsewhere on some foreign land.

The eyes of the nation focused on Florida as an important resource for the readiness that was needed, enhanced to a great degree by politicians such as Senator Claude Pepper who pointed to Florida as a perfect spot for promoting and developing preparedness for the inevitable. Activity mounted with expansions everywhere to help meet the threat of war. Real estate deals were being confirmed for the creation and expansion of military bases across the state and there were real estate changes throughout Florida. Patriotism began to take on an air of importance unlike any other time since World War I.

No Americans, however, could fully appreciate the extent to which a worldwide war would require the ultimate sacrifice of their loved ones' lives. While running for his third election in 1940, President Roosevelt sensed the fears of his electorates and made promises that he would have to break later. In a speech delivered at Boston Garden on October 29, 1940, he sought to appease his constituents with the following promise made at the end of his speech: *"While I am talking to you mothers and fathers, I give you one more assurance. I have said this before but I shall say it again and again and again. Your boys are not going to be sent into any foreign wars."*[15]

*"Your boys are not going to be sent into any foreign wars"* were words that had to be eaten later by the president. They were words of political expediency and he had to do a lot of backtracking as the situation in Europe grew worse and worse. Meanwhile, preparation for war continued in both subtle and obvious ways as the US continued to train allied pilots from other countries and poured money and materials to assist in the fight against the Axis threat.

Florida began witnessing gigantic growth in areas such as

public transportation with WPA projects building and improving highways that crisscrossed the state. Despite the growing threat of war, tourists still flocked to Florida, beckoned by sunshine and the lure of pleasures such as fishing and sunbathing on white sanded beaches. The state's most popular destination was Marineland near St. Augustine and in 1940 Miami drew almost 2 million tourists. Visitors enjoyed treks to such places as Bok Tower in Lake Wales and the Sunken Gardens at St. Petersburg. Florida's rural population was once the majority but changed quickly and Florida became the most urbanized southern state by 1940. Almost two out of three Floridians now lived in cities such as Tampa, Jacksonville or Miami. Florida also had its unique problems at a time when there would be a major influx of newcomers arriving from the north with social mores vastly different from what they had known. Southern traditions, particularly in the rural, central and northern part of the state, were stringently adhered to by dyed-in-the-wool "crackers." One writer made an interesting observation that "politically and socially, Florida has its own North and South but its northern area is strictly southern and its southern area is strictly northern."[16]

  Some diehards were still fighting the Civil War and resisted the great influx of "Yankee" tourists into the state. After all, state holidays in Florida still honored southern heroes, including Robert E. Lee's birthday on January 19th and Confederate Memorial Day on April 26th. Racial tensions ran high. Before 1940 Florida led all states in per capita lynchings and blacks were segregated at every level of social life. There was not a single woman, black or Republican, in the Florida legislature when it convened in 1939. The "good 'ol boys" were known as "porkchoppers" who refused legislation that benefited zones to the south, which leaned toward more liberal views.

  White supremacy was at the heart of Florida's economy and no blacks voted in the Democratic white primary or served on a jury. Senator Claude Pepper, destined to become one of the south's most distinguished statesmen, expressed bigoted sentiment in 1938, an opposite stance to his later beliefs in equal rights:

> *Whatever may be placed upon the statute books of the Nation, however many soldiers may be stationed about the ballot boxes of the Southland, the colored race will not vote, because in so doing so under the present circumstances they endanger the supremacy of a race to which God has committed the destiny of a continent, perhaps of a world.*[17]

(I recall, as a small child, attending a Pepper political rally with my family at the small airport outside of Ellenton. I was quite impressed with the man because I assumed that the free Dr. Pepper sodas had been named after him.)

Many Floridians feared that the influx of radicals from the north might well upset the social scales of segregation adhered to by tradition. Would such prejudices be allowed to continue if the US united its forces against the enemy? Could conscription include blacks as well as whites and would integration be allowed in Florida barracks? In 1940 such changes were thought to be absolutely inconceivable by conservative Floridians who simply could not comprehend the full consequences of a united homeland. In fact, the horrible manner in which African Americans were segregated and given menial jobs by the US government would forever be a blight upon US history and certainly was not restricted to Florida.

No one could have fully anticipated the ultimate consequences aimed at Florida with the impending variety of changes that were coming. Historian Charlton W. Tebeau provides an analysis of Florida's situation:

> *The fifth decade of the twentieth century opened in Florida on a note of recovery and optimism. The*

> *depression was apparently over. The relief and recovery spending and reforming activities of the New Deal had largely ceased. The New Deal left a legacy in greatly increased governmental activity, personnel, and expenditure that created administrative and financial problems with which political leadership had not yet come to grips. Almost unnoticed by Americans, a Second World War was already under way. The stimulus to the American economy reached into Florida. With a somewhat uneasy feeling of security behind their neutrality legislation, most Americans little dreamed that they would be totally involved in that conflict.*[18]

The fact that "a Second World War was already under way" was true and real estate transactions were already soaring in Florida as the government sought to expand the war effort. Rumblings of war could no longer be ignored in Florida and across the US as news flashed across movie screens and mad scenes of European warfare increased with vivid radio news reports and screaming newspaper headlines. By the middle of 1941 FDR had set up an informal agreement with Britain that was called the Atlantic Charter. It provided for "self-determination, freedom of the seas, equal access to world trade and resources, and an end to the use of force in international affairs."[19] The agreement, though not a formal treaty requiring congressional approval, also called for the end to Nazi tyranny.

Several incidents on the high seas involved US ships being fired upon by Nazi submarines and Roosevelt used these incidents to force Congress to pass legislation allowing an undeclared shooting war at sea. Hitler was heavily engaged in the difficult struggle with the Soviet Union at that time and did not wish to openly confront the United States. Therefore, Germany tried to avoid greater confrontation with a nation that was already poised to step in to assist their allies. America's decisions about entering the war were changing steadily and Japan's approaching attack on Pearl Harbor would leave the US no other choice but to denounce neutrality.

On December 3, 1941, the public was shocked to read these headlines in the *Chicago Tribune: F.D.R.'S WAR PLANS*. Chesly Manly, the *Tribune's* Washington correspondent, had printed word-for-word a copy of the so-called *Rainbow Report*, a top war plan drawn up by the joint boards of the US Army and Navy. It was most revealing when he also printed a copy of a secret letter sent by President Roosevelt with a request that the plan be established. It was one of the most embarrassing incidents during FDR's entire tenure as president. The plan called for a 10-million-man army, including a force of 5 million men sent to invade Europe in 1943 to defeat Hitler's war machine. Only a year earlier FDR had promised that no sons would be sent to fight on foreign soil.[20] Many of his most loyal fans were now confused and disappointed. Some even felt betrayed by their beloved leader.

Most Republicans and some Democrats were outraged to think that the president had gone so far as to draw up detailed plans for the war. Numerous Republicans lambasted the president for his secret plot to involve the US in war. Notably among those was Democratic Senator Burton K. Wheeler of Montana who made a radio speech in which he accused the president of having a "New Deal Foreign Policy" that would "plow under every fourth American boy."[21] This accusation was particularly harsh because of the president's backing of a federal plan in the 1930s that paid farmers to plow under crops to create artificial shortages and higher prices. Manly's story was touted in Congress, which recommended that it become part of the Congressional Record.[22] FDR denounced Wheeler's denunciation as "the rottenest thing that has been said in public life in my generation."[23]

Antiwar sentiments ran deep through America at that time.

Even such artists as Pete Seeger and Woody Guthrie joined in the protest movement against war. They had previously featured a song, *Plow Under*, which underscored pubic dissension over federal policies under FDR that favored the plowing in of crops and this song immediately became a rallying cry for neutrality and resistance to New Deal war policies.

The average household, like that of most everyone I knew during my own childhood, adored FDR and, for the most part, supported his policies. He was given credit for pulling America out of the Great Depression. In Florida, electricity was installed in most homes, roads were improved and poverty was eradicated. Low and middle-class Floridians almost believed that he was God's gift to humanity and that possibly he was responsible for the rising and the setting of the sun. His picture hung on the walls of many homes in my community and was proudly displayed in our classrooms next to Presidents Washington and Abraham Lincoln.

Residents in Florida, like those across the US, wanted to believe that it would be possible to live in peace without involvement in the world's problems. But it is incomprehensible that anyone could deny that FDR was forthright in his commitment to the cause of its American allies. True, he definitely tried to appease his critics with his political maneuvering but his fireside chats and other speeches made it absolutely clear that his beloved country was facing the inevitability of war. His leadership was increasingly convincing enough to appease most of his leading critics. Indeed, the revelation of the so-called war plans on December 4, 1941, came only a week before the attack on Pearl Harbor, an event so powerful that Americans were finally forced to accept President Roosevelt's assessment of the times. Pearl Harbor would be the awakening call that would shake Americans out of their lethargy to the reality of a new day and age that would forever alter their lives. Indeed, a nation at war would play a very

## Jim Wiggins

major role in the lives of Floridians who would soon be immersed in unimaginable changes

# Chapter Two

# War is Declared

It was the afternoon of December 7, 1941. I was 11 years-old. My mother had invited our Sunday school class to our home in Ellenton for a taffy pull. I was sitting on the back steps with a wad of sticky candy with friends and my brother, Richard, age 13, when Aunt Myrtle came running over from next door. Aunt Myrtle was often in a dither about something but this time she was overly excited, almost hysterical, as she announced the news she had just heard on the radio. A place called Pearl Harbor had just been bombed by Japanese planes. She was sobbing uncontrollably because of her concern about her son, DeWayne, who was in the Navy.

Where was Pearl Harbor? No one seemed to know. Aunt Myrtle had recently heard from our cousin with a recording that said he was stationed at a place called New Caledonia. Was it near Pearl Harbor? My dad led Aunt Myrtle back home to look up the location in the World Atlas, assuring his sister that his nephew was nowhere near where the bombers had struck. The impact of the Japanese attack had taken on personal concerns but few of us acknowledged the wider significance of what was actually taking place. We could not comprehend the implications involved in such a thing as war. We were simply a group of adolescents whose partying had been abruptly disturbed by a message that we could not digest. It was only when I saw the tears streaming down the face of my mother that I finally surmised that something highly significant had taken place.

Meanwhile, my mother dipped out the last of the taffy into waiting hands and instructed everyone that the party would soon be over. A short time later everyone climbed into the back of the pickup and Dad delivered them to their homes where they found parents sitting around their radios listening to the latest reports about the Pearl Harbor attacks. I thought it quite strange that several of the parents came out to the truck and hugged their children as though they had been away on a trip. Tears flowed freely and it was a very intense trip through the neighborhood as friends of my father stopped him to talk about an incident that, obviously, was to affect our future lives in a very adverse manner. The peaceful little community of Ellenton would never be the same and Florida, in particular, would play a significant role like none other in the United States. But for most of us the war years would just be the era required of every kid whose only task was to grow up. It was no big deal. That was just the way it was. War or not, we were destined to do only what came naturally. Kids would still be kids.

I remember sitting with my parents near the radio the next afternoon, December 8, when President Roosevelt made his famous speech to Congress. It began with "Yesterday, December 7, 1941...a date which will live in infamy...the United America was suddenly and deliberately attacked by naval and air forces of the empire of Japan."[1] He went on to state that it was obvious, due to the distance between Japan and Hawaii, that Japan had planned the attack for days or weeks while trying to deceive the US. War, he said, had "been thrust upon the United States" and the US had not been the aggressor.

I remember watching my mother wipe away tears as she and Dad sat holding hands. Afterward, I remember Aunt Myrtle

Photo 2 - Headlines in newspapers across Florida screamed the news of the Pearl Harbor Attack on December 7, 1941. This headline in the Tallahassee News-Democrat was a special edition. *(Florida Archives)*

calling across from next door to discuss what the president had said, relieved in a sense that her son was hundreds of miles away from the scene of Pearl Harbor, but still overly concerned about his presence on a ship somewhere in the waters of the Pacific. She hoped that he wasn't near the Philippines or some other island that was also attacked by the Japanese. Her other son, Kline, had also announced his intentions and restlessly anticipated joining up as soon as he graduated from high school. Extreme anxiety seemed to permeate every household in our small community and no one could fully anticipate the impact that the war would have upon our lives.

## Jim Wiggins

The resolution by Congress declaring war was passed with one dissenting vote. Summations by commentators about the speech include the following:

> *The speech was over in six minutes and war voted in less than an hour, but the real job was done in the first ten seconds. 'Infamy' was the real note that struck home, the word that welded the country together until the war was won.*[2]

The word "infamy," of course, was not in the average person's vocabulary in 1941. Even our teacher at the elementary school in Ellenton had to look up the word in class when we discussed the speech and its implications for us. She took out the dictionary and read the words of meaning and we were left with the idea that the attack was something that was particularly demonizing, feeling quite at ease with the teacher's derogatory use of the word "Japs" when referring to these invading perpetrators of evil. Of course, we had all been indoctrinated by the media long before the president's speech. Up until this time the ultimate threat had been the Germans and it was not at all unusual to see kids on the playground doing a silly goosestep to mimic the comical Hitler and his soldiers. The swastika symbol of hate was now being augmented by the addition of the rising sun of Japan, while the Fascist name of Mussolini never really seemed to occupy a significant place of importance since few of us understood the Italian threat.

Servicemen from all over the US, including many from Florida, would later describe their own personal experience at Pearl Harbor on that eventful day when the Japanese flew in low through the mountain ranges. Raymond Medved of Bradenton said that he was fortunate in being transferred to the USS Philadelphia "right before everything went down. I was blessed, and I will never forget those soldiers." Bill Russell of Holmes Beach, a seaman second class aboard the USS Sacramento, recalls

## Jim Wiggins

"They blew the hell out of the place, that's what I remember most." He had been running harbor patrol six months prior to the bombing and remembered waking up with all the commotion. "I hit the deck, and the planes had big red circles on their wings. I saw some soldiers with no gun stations throwing potatoes at the planes, that's how close those planes were. I saw every dive bomber and every torpedo plane, stayed aboard ship and fired guns at them, dropping shells. I can still see those red circles and the faces inside the cockpits."[3]

Jack Copess of Bradenton was working as a shipfitter under a contract attaching radar on destroyers at Pearl Harbor. He said, "I had worked forty-nine days straight, putting in 12 and 16 hours a day. I told the foreman I needed a day off." He got Sunday off and was ten miles east of the bombing when his landlady rushed in to tell him to tune in on the radio to hear about the attack. "I remember rushing down to the beach, seeing the wave of torpedo planes." He continued, "Those Japanese bombers made one big mistake because the resolve in this country was really hardened by that attack, and we knew where they lived." He also remembers that he and his buddies kept singing "Yankee Doodle Dandy" after the 6 p.m. curfew in the days that followed so that no one would mistake them for enemies.[4]

On December 11 Germany and Italy declared war on the United States. There was no turning back. By this time Floridians were already becoming immersed in real estate transactions that were mapping out the use of its flat open land for military bases. Everything was happening fast. No lives in Florida would ever be the same. But for barefoot kids like myself, the war years would just be another part of growing up and doing what came naturally in a pristine environment that offered all the amenities necessary to insure a happy and well adjusted childhood. After all, we were facing the frightening experience of our adolescent and teenage years and it was hard to imagine how anything such as a war could disrupt that. There were still tree houses to be built, tin canoes to be fashioned and skinny dipping to be enjoyed in the creeks, shell pits and the Manatee River. Puberty, peer pressure and the full awakening to the opposite sex were far too pressing to fully interrupt those important years with anything so mundane as a war being fought somewhere else.

Photo 3 - Crowds filled a school in Leon County in 1940 when registration for Selective Service began. Men between the ages of 21 to 36 were required to sign up for the Draft. *(Florida Archives)*

# Chapter Three

# Florida's Military Bases

Florida was soon saturated with military bases. No area on Florida's soil was overlooked as a possible site for building more and more bases, which would soon be thickly sprinkled about the peninsula. Expediency was essential. Sites were increasingly pinpointed on Federal chart boards in growing numbers as the intensity of war increased. Almost everyone soon lived close to some new installation. No kid in Florida was immune to the increasing numbers of aircraft droning overhead in squadrons, nor would they be surprised to encounter convoys of trucks on their highways. Indeed, every aspect of life was rapidly changing.

I recall how fascinated we became in watching squadrons of planes flying overhead in formation and I remember more than one occasion when our school bus pulled over to the side of the road to allow a convoy to pass by with soldiers waving and throwing kisses at the teenage girls hanging out the windows. Such scenes were very common for all of us and we simply learned to take it in stride. Increasingly, many friends and relatives had the difficult task of saying goodbye to loved ones. There was soon a shortage of young men in every neighborhood.

The establishment of military bases was paramount to the US war efforts. Florida was to have a vast array of airfields and military installations unlike anywhere else in the world. And it all began long before the bombing of Pearl Harbor in 1941 and the declaration of war by Congress and FDR. As indicated, when the advent of World War II began on September 1, 1939, in Europe with the bombing of Poland by German Ju-87s, it became apparent that US leadership take notice, particularly when Britain and France declared war two days later. America was no longer anchored in its declaration of neutrality but, rather, accepted the pressing need to accelerate its efforts to strengthen every aspect of its war efforts. Particular attention was given toward aviation strength, which was an immediate priority.

The invasion of Poland unveiled the German *blitzkrieg*, which combined massive air power with rapidly moving armored units. This show of force spotlighted American deficiencies during the period of the Neutrality Act and the Federal Government recognized the absolute necessity of strengthening its allied air power. Only 500 pilots a year were being trained at the Randolph Field in Texas before the declaration of war. This was a mere drop in the bucket if the US was to participate fully in the challenges of a new brutal world war.[1]

England could not stand alone in its fight against Germany at a time when the Luftwaffe flew freely over its channel and airfields, almost totally wiping out its squadrons and bombers. Aircraft were being destroyed in large numbers and pilots needed training to man new planes. Time was of the essence and the US could not idly stand by and do nothing. In late 1940 there was a top-ranking meeting in New York of experts from the US, Britain and Canada to discuss what could be done to alleviate the loss of allied air power. Despite the Neutrality Act, the delegation decided that it would set up training schools for pilots in the US. A variety of fighter and bomber aircraft would be used and then it would be up to the pilots to return to their home country to join in the fight. Thus, Florida became a major destination for such training:

> *Arriving in small numbers at first, they came from Australia, England, Canada, India, China, South Africa, Norway, Czechoslovakia, Greece, France,*

Photo 4 - British cadets and their instructors pose outside their aircraft at Carlstrom Field in 1940 at Arcadia. *(Florida Archives)*

> *Brazil and Poland. Many of the pilots from the British Empire wore the uniform of the RAF, which included many trainees from Poland and Greece. They were shipped to Embry-Riddle schools at Dorr and Carlstrom airfields, to Greenville Aviation at Ocala, Lodwick Aviation Academy at Lakeland, Riddle-McKayAero College at Clewiston and the Orlando Aero School. All*

> *these schools shared in training the eager young Allies.*[2]

Allied schools were being held at Arcadia and elsewhere throughout the state, including intermediate training sites. In 1940 a large group of military personnel from Central and South America arrived for training at the Embry-Riddle School at Miami. Allied training in Florida prepared more men at its bases than at any others of the 62 civilian school and 150 military facilities in the entire US Despite this flagrant activity by the US, Germany dared not take on the Americans at that time. In fact, Russian trainees also arrived, when Germany decided to invade their homeland.

Hap Arnold, General of the Army Air Force, called together a group of World War I veterans and a few civilian flyers to draw up plans to overhaul the flight training program. Florida, of course, was to have a major role in these plans. Cadet flight training schools were conducted at civilian operated airfields that offered about 10 weeks of ground instruction and over 60 hours of flight training. Seven of these schools were located in Florida. They included the Greenville Aviation School at Ocala, the Lodwick Schools at Lakeland and Avon Park, the Riddle-McKay Aero College at Clewiston, the Embry-Riddle Schools at Dorr and the Carlstom fields at Arcadia. There were also air schools at Winter Park and Miami.

Governor Spessard Holland was a veteran and supported major plans for installment and enlargement of bases on Florida land. Again, Senator Claude Pepper convinced Congress that Florida was better suited for air bases than any other state because of its flat surface and open land. He also pointed out that railroads ran up and down both coasts and crisscrossed the state, making it easy for the transportation of troops and war materials.

## Jim Wiggins

Movement for increased US military prowess was already under way during the pre-war years but Congress absolutely could not wait any longer after the bombing of Pearl Harbor, which dissolved the Neutrality Act. They instantly enacted a program known as the Development of Landings Areas for National Defense (DLA) and together with the Civil Aviation Agency (CAA) and the military, proceeded to select sites suitable to meet the needs of the country during wartime.

Senator Pepper, with other influential Floridians and local

Photo 5 - British Royal Navy pilots arrive for training in 1940 at the Pensacola Naval Air Station. *(Florida Archives)*

business groups, quickly persuaded the CAA of the many benefits of locating military bases, especially airfields, in Florida. Many airports already existed in Florida and these communities were eager to offer them to the military. With CAA funds, barracks, hangars, sewage treatment facilities, housing, administration and other buildings were rapidly added. Local contractors employed increasing numbers of workers in their rush to meet the demand of the needed military bases. Florida was in a hurry everywhere.[3]

Indeed, Florida was in a hurry. The years of the war were a boom to Florida's sluggish pre-war economy but now the race was on to accomplish what would have been thought impossible earlier, encouraged at all times by President Roosevelt's challenge to do the impossible like the little red train engine that succeeded in spite of the odds.

Florida was quickly divided into two areas by the Stratmeyer Towers Conference in early 1942.

> *The Army would develop its airfields on the western half and the Navy on the eastern half. This arrangement satisfied both branches, as it did not include existing facilities such as Jacksonville, Pensacola, MacDill, and Key West. The Army later violated the agreement by building Morrison Air Base at Palm Beach.*[4]

By the end of the war there were 227 bases in Florida. This was an astronomical number, particularly when one considers that there were only six bases in Florida prior to the war years. What an enormous change for the Sunshine State! Bases were scattered from one end of the state to the other...and in between. Almost every citizen in Florida could claim proximity to a military establishment of some kind. Convoys of trucks crowded every highway, squadrons of planes flew overhead and servicemen stood on street corners waiting for a lift home or back to their base after furlough. No one in Florida was immune to the presence of war in their own backyard.

It must suffice, however, to give only a brief glimpse of military bases in Florida during the war years. Each base, in its own way, had distinctive qualities and it is likely that volumes could be written if space would allow such. Many of the 227 bases were actually auxiliary bases and in many instances names were changed during and after the war. For the purpose of this writing, the names used will be those assigned during the war years. Men who lived in the barracks of primitive bases would likely have enough negative comments to fill up thousands of pages on each individual one. In several instances their comments are included, particularly from those who had to endure living in tents during inclement weather without heat or suitable plumbing. Though humorous, some comments would not pass censorship for these pages, particularly from those assigned from out of state to Florida's tropical setting that was not at all compatible with previous living conditions. Here, then, is a limited glimpse of Florida's numerous bases that played significant roles in America's Second World War. For clarity's sake, the bases are divided into geographical locations.

**Northeast Florida.**

The Naval Air Station (NAS) in Jacksonville served as a very important training ground for pilots. Originally, the Jacksonville Municipal Airport was temporarily used, particularly in the search for U-boats which were freely raising havoc along Florida's Atlantic coastline. Jacksonville quickly developed dozens of fields and training schools for thousands, including a few blimps, which were used for detecting German submarines offshore.

Camp Blanding has quite a long history, which reaches back to 1907 when 300 acres were acquired at Black Point through the efforts of citizens at a cost of less than seven thousand dollars. An additional 400 acres were added prior to World War I and were used as a rifle range and training facility for troops living in tents. In the late 1930s it served as the training facility for the Florida National Guard and was known as Camp Foster. In 1939 the Navy wanted to establish a facility near Jacksonville on the St. Johns River so a land swap deal was made. A 30,000-acre site, nine miles east of Starke in Clay County, was chosen as the National Guard setting and this was the beginning of Camp Blanding, a base that would eventually become the fourth-largest city in Florida at the height of its existence. Military employees, the WPA, and local contractors moved with haste to build and develop on the expanded land area acquired by purchase and lease, a major enterprise that provided facilities for more than 70,000 military personnel at one time. Brigadier General Ralph W. Cooper, Jr. had this to say:

*Thus begun a mobilization center and training site used by the Army throughout World War II. Its 170,000 acres of scrub oaks and thickets and the training of some 90,000 enlistees at its peak made Camp Blanding the fourth largest city in Florida. Between the war years of 1940-1945, more than 800,000 enlistees and draftees received their military training at Blanding. A Prisoner of War Compound was established east of the service area. It was maintained until the prisoners were repatriated following the war. German and Italian POWs were maintained in separate compounds.* [5]

## Jim Wiggins

Most of the POWs at Camp Blanding had been captured in North Africa and France. Many were then fanned out throughout the state into agricultural areas which desperately needed labor for growing and harvesting of food, which was an important part of the war cause. (Additional information about these prison camps is offered elsewhere.)

Camp Blanding was one of the most familiar names for everyone in Florida since so many young men were assigned there after their induction into the Army. My friends and I heard the

Photo 6 - This aerial view of a portion of Camp Blanding includes the hospital complex. *(Florida Archives)*

name spoken often by family members and residents of the community. It seemed as if almost everyone knew someone who was stationed there. I'm not sure that most of us knew where it was but we certainly heard reports about it from friends and relatives returning on furlough after boot camp. Of course, this also included a lot of complaining.

Dredging began in 1940 at Ribault Bay in Mayport at the site of 700 acres on the mouth of the St. Johns River It was completed a year later and became an auxiliary naval air station that was designed to refuel and rearm fighter aircraft from other bases. An aircraft carrier provided a site for training pilots to land and take off. Many PT boats received their training at Mayport and the Coast Guard maintained a patrol facility there during the German submarine crisis of 1942.

Twelve hundred enlisted men were stationed at Melborne's Naval Air Station that was designed to service aircraft. It was also a base for WAVES and contained 300 German POWs toward the close of the war in 1945. Gunnery pilots were also trained there and an outlying field at Valkaria near Malabar was a

Photo 7 - Men from Company M, 124th Infantry, join in maneuvers at Camp Blanding. *(Florida Archives)*

small airfield that trained pilots for carrier landings with the use of catapult and landing arresting gear

Vero Beach Naval Air Station offered a unique service as a night training base. 1,700 enlisted men and 300 officers were housed there and two units participated in training as fighter pilots. Many were lost in the difficult night maneuvers that often took them to other fields. An air-sea rescue unit at Fort Pierce was often called upon to search for downed pilots.

The Banana River Naval Air Station was located on 1,824 acres just south of Cocoa Beach and served as a seaplane base.

## Jim Wiggins

PBM flying boats patrolled the Atlantic for submarines in 1940-41 but these were replaced with Kingfishers in 1942. The facility also housed a blimp, which was used for German submarine surveillance. The site also housed an aerial photography school, a navigational school, and was a repair depot, housing 2,500 enlisted men and 390 officers at its peak.

An auxiliary field housed the NAS Dive Bombing Training School which was at Cecil Field, located 16 miles below Jacksonville. Navy pilots were trained to land on carrier decks and pilots practiced gunnery and bomb dives on nearby targets at Mill Cove, Amelia City, Black Creek, Chafe, and elsewhere on Florida's scrub land which was found suitable. Like elsewhere throughout Florida, many trainees crashed on training maneuvers and were killed.

Fort Pierce witnessed the offshore sinking of many allied ships by German U-boats and served as a rescue and hospitalization treatment center for survivors. Events in the South Pacific and the threat of invasions on the shores of Europe inspired the US to open the Naval Amphibious Training Base in early 1943. Trainees received instruction in amphibious landing techniques and included combat engineers, Navy Seabees, scouts and demolition teams. The setting was ideal, including both the Indian River lagoon and the ocean. The training led to preparation for upcoming invasions such as that in Europe at Normandy.

Green Cove Springs, located on the west bank of the St. Johns River below Jacksonville, was an auxiliary US Navy base, the site of Lee Field, which trained pilots on four 5,000-foot runways. Barracks held 600 officers and 2,000 enlisted men who were primarily instructed in gunnery warfare that would provide cover for ground troops on Pacific Islands. Attack training took place at Chafe, Amelia City, Black Creek, and Palatka.

Daytona Beach Naval Air Station was the site of a pilot training program that sent men into direct combat overseas. Four nearby fields were located at Tonoka in Ormond Beach, Bunnell, New Smyrna Beach and Spruce Creek. The sites included catapult and arresting gear maneuvers and gunnery training schools.

## Northwest Florida

The presence of the US Navy in Pensacola goes way back to 1826 when a base was constructed just south of the city. Nearby were the Army bases of Fort McRee, Fort Barancas and The Redoubt. The Navy abandoned the navy yard during the Civil War when it was captured by the Confederates but Union troops continued to hold Fort Pickens on nearby Santa Rosa Island throughout the Civil War. In 1862 the Navy Yard was re-occupied by Federal troops and served as a base for Admiral Farragut's fleet in the blockage of Mobile Bay.

By 1938 the US Navy had once again established itself with its Pensacola Air station and with time, including its auxiliary stations, was capable of training nearly 1,000 pilots each month. Correy Field, three miles north, had a field on 500 acres of land, which consisted of two separate airways, known as the East or West fields. One runway was 4,200 feet in length and served as a strip for training allied personnel before the US declaration of war. By mid-1944 some 200 officers and 1,600 enlisted personnel were stationed at Corry, with 400 to 500 students.[6] The special flight training school of Navy Flight Surgeons was also located there.

A seaplane air base was built at Perdido Bay and commissioned as Bronson Field in November of 1942. Two outlying bases were located in nearby Alabama for additional training and emergency landings. Ellyson was also an auxiliary base for NAS Pensacola, located about seven miles away. It served primarily to train aviators in the use of the Vultee SNV Valiant, better known as the "Vultee Vibrator," a difficult craft that had a two-stage propeller that vibrated.

Panama City was the site of a naval amphibious training

base and was the primary training ground for the Civil Air Patrol. Tyndall Army Air Field was used for training Army gunnery bomber crews and was perhaps one of the more interesting sites because of the manner in which aircraft practiced shooting live ammunition at sleeve tow-targets behind other aircraft such as the AT-trainer planes. These practice missions used changing colored

Photo 8 - A parade and review is held at the Dale Mabry Air Field in Tallahassee. *(Florida Archives)*

targets and provided local people aerial shows like nowhere else in Florida. Outsiders would line the highways on the outskirts of the base to watch the cat-and-mouse performances in the air above them.

Eglin Army Air Field and its ten auxiliary fields was an extremely important base for the Army Air Corps and it was here that Colonel James Doolittle trained his men for the raid on Tokyo toward the end of the war. The base is located about fifty miles east of Pensacola near the communities of Niceville and Valpariso. The Army used this base as a testing ground for aircraft armaments and equipment, which required space for a bombing and gunnery range.

Eglin had an extensive history and before World War I served as the Air Corps Specialized Flying School and became a proving ground with auxiliary fields developed nearby during the war. In 1935 Maxwell Field in Alabama leased the airport as its headquarters for an air base, which expanded during the 1930s and was ultimately designed to be one of the most important US Air Force bases during World War II.

Tallahassee's Dale Mabry Army Air Field (today's site of the Tallahassee Community College) was the training grounds for

Photo 9 - Florida National Guardsmen Participate In Maneuvers At National Bridge In Leon County. *(Florida Archives)*

the famous Tuskeegee Airmen, the black pilots who fought so courageously in their dilapidated P-47s to escort US bombers through enemy fire toward the end of the war in 1944-45. (This was at a time when black servicemen were segregated, given menial jobs and watched German POWs being given better treatment than they.)

Between Pensacola and Tallahassee was the Marianna Army Air Base. Trainers were sent there in 1942 from the Maxwell AAF in Montgomery, Ala., and five auxiliary fields were built in and around Marianna to provide training for pilots of fighter aircraft.

## Jim Wiggins

Camp Gordon Johnson was the largest facility in the Panhandle during the war and, perhaps, was one of the most unpopular, particularly during its earliest beginnings in 1942. Even General Omar Bradley was quoted as complaining, "The man who selected that site should have been court-martialed for stupidity."[7]

Ten thousand acres were purchased and another 150,000

Photo 10 - Men wait in the chow line at Camp Gordon Johnson in 1943. (*Florida Archives*)

acres were leased and clearing began on July 8, 1942, at a place called Carrabelle, Fla. Four separate camp facilities were being carved out of wilderness land, one for the Amphibious Training Center and the others for the three regimental combat teams. Dog and St. George islands lay just offshore and the various beaches between Alligator Point and St. George's Island were utilized for amphibious landing and training areas. Airborne troops were also trained at Carrabelle.

Those who arrived at Carrabelle in September of 1942

## Jim Wiggins

were not happy campers and complained that the facilities were the worst in the nation. Captain James J. Cuffee described it this way:

> We all thought we had it made...palm trees and warm breezes from the Gulf. None of us knew where Carrabelle was. What a hell hole that was! It was worse than anything I had ever seen, even worse than the CCC camps were. Let me tell you, they were rustic, but this was worse. Latrines were poor and every time it rained, and it did that most of the time, everything just oozed to the surface of the ground. It stunk real badly for weeks! My platoon lived in nine-man tents and it was damned cold. Those poor guys in the barracks were no better off, even with pot bellied stoves. Most tents and barracks didn't even have wooden floors or platforms, just dirt. When it rained it was terrible. Everything was mud...We ate outdoors in the good ole chow line with mess kits. The food was terrible.[8]

Cuffee went on to describe how they spent weeks digging and trying to clear away the scrub brush. Some local contractors assisted in the building of barracks but their work was shoddy. He continued:

> All the time you were working, those stinking chiggers, sand flies or mosquitoes ate you alive. I think the chiggers were the worst insects I had ever met. They got in where your clothing fit tight, like around your belt and feasted on your blood. I used to rub ammonia water on me to take away the itch, an old trick a mountain man taught me in Montana, but my pals didn't care for the smell. When they found out how well it worked, we all smelled of ammonia.[9]

He went on to talk about the great abundance of

rattlesnakes and the presence of wild hogs in camp as they trained on obstacle courses with pillboxes and other offensive and defensive maneuvers. Of course, the presence of red bugs (chiggers), sand flies, mosquitoes and rattlesnakes is something with which all of us lived back in those days when Florida was pristine. It was just something that we accepted as part of Florida's great outdoors. But newcomers evidently found it to be particularly excruciating.

Lake City is located in north central Florida and the Naval Air Station included a repair hanger, ammunition storage bunkers, barracks, three 6,000-foot runways, one 7,000-foot runway and auxiliary fields at nearby Lake Butler, Cedar Key, Alachua and Gainesville. Training was primarily for the PV-1 Ventura which was used so effectively against enemy submarines during the war.

**Central Florida.**

Melbourne's Naval Air Station was used for gunnery training but also served as a base for Navy WAVES. Fort Pierce had the US Naval Amphibious Training Base and joint services for Army and Navy personnel. It was also the site of an underwater demolition facility. Orlando had the Army Air School and training for the Civilian Pilot Training program. Also, it was the instructional base for an amphibious squadron group. Nearby Rollins College operated a flight training school and utilized the nearby auxiliary fields for practice.

As indicated, army air schools were desperate for pilots just prior to the war and schools were set up at Ocala, Lakeland, Avon Park and Arcadia. Each of these schools was highly successful and all of them expanded during the early 1940s to meet the increasing demand, not only for the allies from overseas, but also for US trainees.

Hendricks Army Air Field in Sebring was home to the heavy B-17 bombers and housed 225 officers and 2,456 enlisted men. Some of the B-17s reportedly carried depth charges, which were dropped on German U-boats in the Atlantic. Gunnery training and bombing raids took place at Naples and Avon Park and it was estimated that as many as 7,000 landings and takeoffs took place at Hendricks within a given week.[10]

St. Petersburg was close to Tampa's McDill Air Force Base and provided the US with four air bases of its own. In 1939 the Coast Guard began its air station at Albert Whitted Field and also operated an air-sea rescue mission station at Bayboro Harbor (future site of Eckerd College).

A federal commission appointed by the US War

Photo 11 - This memorial stands in Arcadia to honor 23 British RAF cadets who lost their lives while training in Florida. *(Florida Archives)*

Department in 1939 selected Tampa to be the site for the MacDill Army Air Base. It was located on 5,800 acres of land, including 3.500 donated by Hillsborough County at Catfish Point. The WPA began clearing the land and the base officially opened on April 15, 1941. Two other fields, Henderson (where Busch

## Jim Wiggins

Gardens is today) and Drew (presently Tampa International Airport) were also there and served as auxiliary fields. MacDill was a transitional training facility with cadres from the 29th and 44th Bombardment Group flying B-17s. (It was not unusual at all for nearby squadrons of B-17s to be seen flying on training

Photo 12 - P-51D Mustangs wait for takeoff at MacDill Army Air Base in Tampa for joint American, British, and French aerial training and operations. *(Florida Archives)*

missions over my hometown of Ellenton during my teen years.)

Some 15,000 troops were stationed at MacDill and a large contingent of WACS served there. Nearby Zephryhills and Brooksville had auxiliary fields that served MacDill as needed and Passage Key, Mullet Key, Terra Ceia, South Venice and Osprey provided gunnery and bombing ranges. Many residents, including myself, watched the bombing practice flights at Passage Key in the Gulf waters just north of Anna Maria Island.

A cadre from MacDill also established a training base on 900 acres at Bartow. The airfield also served as an emergency landing strip. The Army Air Force Base at Lakeland included five squadrons of the 98th Bombardment Group, which used fields in Tampa, Osprey and Avon Park as bombsites. The nearby Lokwick School was first designed to train US pilots but later began training for British RAF pilot cadets.

Training for outstanding college students was provided by the Civilian Pilot Training program at Rollins College in Winter Park and the Orlando Army Air Force was the home base for two amphibious units. Nearby Cannon Mills, Pine Castle, and Holquist were training fields and emergency landing strips.

## Southeast Florida

Palm Beach and West Palm Beach had Coast Guard and Army facilities for women and provided headquarters for the Air Transport Command for the Caribbean. In October of 1941 the 313th Material Squadron was transferred from the Miami Municipal Airport to Morrison Field in West Palm Beach and was hastily set up with troops being housed in tents that were flooded out with heavy rains in April of 1942.

## Jim Wiggins

This site was responsible for maintaining airport facilities and the aircraft of the Ferry Command.

Traffic was very heavy in 1943-44 with planes being overhauled, repaired and tested for flight. Visitors to the area included the Duke of Windsor and Prince Bernhardt of the Netherlands who had his aircraft repaired there. Over 1,000 men worked three shifts at Morrison Field to meet the heavy demands.

Photo 13 - Navy pilots pose at Fort Lauderdale Naval Air Station, July, 1943. President George H.W. Bush, who learned to fly Grumman TBF Avenger torpedo bombers, is standing in the back row, second from right. *(NAS Fort Lauderdale H.A. Museum)*

Some of these men were even sent to Homestead to train men there in the maintaining and repair of aircraft. Two hundred fifty WACS also held jobs at Morrison and reportedly fit right in beside the men in doing repairs and maintenance.

The Boca Raton Air Base began operations in the summer of 1942 and continued to grow until it reached a capacity of 16,000 troops by 1945. It specialized in radar training taught by highly skilled experts in the field who directed the installing and use of systems into old aircraft during the beginning stages, followed by training for use on the modern aircraft such as B-24s,

B-17s, B-20s, and B-25s. This base was the only radar training center during World War II and offered specialized operations that became vital to success overseas with its squadrons of radar-equipped bombers.

    The Naval Air Station in Ft. Lauderdale was one of the bases where former President George Bush received his pilot training as an ensign. The station consisted of four 5,000-foot asphalt runways and had an emergency grass strip at nearby Davie. Trainees were rotated frequently and were primarily trained as crewmember and pilots for the Grumman TBF and TBM. Target practice was held on North Beach with .59 caliber machine guns firing at moving targets towed by US aircraft. Port Everglades was also the location of a Coast Guard Station and housed Navy ammunitions.

## Jim Wiggins

The Homestead Air Force Base began its operations when a cadre from crowded Morrison Field in West Palm Beach moved there during the late summer of 1942. This base was used as an overflow of aircraft, including fighters and bombers from other bases of the Caribbean Wing, which were then moved to the

Photo 14 - Army Air Corp soldiers receive training on the white sands of Miami Beach. (*Florida Archives*)

Middle East via South America and East Africa, or on to India and China. The base was later hit by a hurricane in 1945 and was temporarily closed.

Miami housed the Replacement Training Center for enlisted men of the Army Air Corp and also had a Coast Guard Air Station. The Naval Air Force on Dinner Key provided support for the transport ferry planes, which flew throughout Florida, the Caribbean and South America. Also, PT boats were trained there. The NAS at Dinner Key housed about 150 officers and 600 enlisted men and trained an average of 650 men at one time.

The Naval Reserve Training Base at Opa Locka became known as NAS Miami and had three fields: Opa Locka, Miami Municipal Airport, and Master Field. It was a large complex with 700 officers and 7,200 enlisted personnel. Two hundred WAVES were stationed there and many served as gunnery instructors at the Naval Air Gunnery School. There was a large repair and maintenance unit and the base also provided fighter and dive bomber training. Practice areas included Florida Bay and other

Photo 15 - US Navy dive-bombers fly over the city of Miami. (*Florida Archives*)

waters of the Florida Keys.

Key West had been a naval base since 1823 and remained in Union hands during the Civil War. During the Spanish American War, it served as an important base in the war waged in Cuba and in 1917 was expanded to include a training site for pilots. In 1939 there was major expansion with the inclusion of airfields on nearby Boca Chica Key and Meacham Field. A seaplane base was also built at Trumbo Point. The Key West units played major roles in the anti-submarine efforts. A 10,000-foot airstrip at Marathon was added but the entire operation became known simply as NAS Key West and included a Coast Guard patrol base, Marine barracks and a Navy submarine base.

One of the most interesting bases in Florida was the Naval Air Station Richmond, which was located about 15 miles southwest of Miami on 2,107 acres of land. Three large, 16-story hangars 270-feet wide by 1,000-feet long housed 14 inflated blimps and 11 deflated blimps, in addition to 366 airplanes and 150 automobiles. Several thousand Naval Air Station personnel were also housed there. It, like the blimp facility at Key West that began a year earlier, was designed in 1941 to patrol the waters offshore when German submarines were increasingly on the prowl.

The Blimp Patrol Squadron ZP-21 was the third-largest blimp base of the four used and had 15 K-sized airships. Some of these were deployed to such places as Key West, San Julian, Banana River and the Isle of Ines in South Carolina. Their mission extended almost down to Cuba and many lives were rescued after sinkings from German submarines. The mere presence of blimps on surveillance missions served as deterrents to the surfacing of submarines, which knew of their presence overhead. Their existence prompted historian Charlton W. Tebeau to acknowledge them as one of the most important deterrents to U-boat activity in Florida waters. He writes: "Lighter-than-air craft that hovered over the area proved the most effective means of detecting submarines in the shallow offshore waters of Florida."[11] Each blimp was armed with an average of four depth charges and a machine gun. It had two engines and reached speeds of about 75 miles an hour and when deflated, could fit into a crate measuring 6 by 12 feet.

The base was later wiped out by a hurricane that roared through on Sept. 15, 1945. Actually, most of the destruction was caused by a fire that was ignited when debris hit the gas tank of an airplane. Ironically, 360 aircraft had been flown there for protection from the winds and were also destroyed in the fire. The base fire chief was the only one who died in the tragedy that ended a special era in US warfare.

## Southwest Florida

Sarasota, Venice, Punta Gorda, Fort Myers, and Naples all had Army Airfields. Sarasota-Manatee County Municipal Airport was leased in 1942 as an official Army base and WPA crews moved in quickly to establish quarters but early living conditions in tents were far from being comfortable. The 97th Bombardment Group was transferred from MacDill to Sarasota in March of 1942 and the newly made double-asphalt and concrete runways had to be strong enough to handle the heavy B-17s. Two months later the 92nd Bomb Group arrived and the Army Air Force base became very busy with several thousand officers assigned there to give training to the rapidly growing numbers of trainees. By June the site was officially listed as an auxiliary base of MacDill when it was decided that the runways were not sufficient for the B-17s. The 92nd was transferred elsewhere and the 69th Fighter Squadron was moved from Drew Field to Sarasota. The 49th also flew the P-39 Aircobra there.

In nearby Punta Gorda there was an airfield that became a submarine-base for Sarasota but was later changed to become a unit under the Army Air Base in Venice, which provided accommodations for 4.000 personnel in its service schools operated by the 27th Service Group.

The community of Ellenton was located between MacDill in Tampa and the air base in Sarasota so the skies were often filled with the drones of B-17s and other aircraft flying between the two sites. Many households had airplane identification charts and residents made it a pastime to look up and identify the particular aircraft that were flying over at the time. A friend of mine was quite knowledgeable and enjoyed pointing out the differences and similarities of aircrafts. My uncle who lived next door and was a retired pilot from World War I took great joy in sharing information about these giant birds that filled the Florida skies during those exciting years.

Civil Air Patrol units were stationed at both Sarasota and Fort Myers. These patrols were organized in late 1941 for the purpose of offering civilian pilots a chance to help in the surveillance of Gulf waters in search of German submarines. Small aircraft such as Cessnas, Wacos, Stinsons and Pipers were used. Some were even privately owned. At one point the operation was referred to as a "Scarecrow Patrol," designed merely to scare away enemy vessels. CAP grew in popularity and in 1941 there were 128,360 certified civilian pilots with more than 14,000 aircraft being flown from more than 2,500 small airfields across Florida.[12] Perry G. Snell, Jr., president of the volunteers at Sarasota wrote:

> *Shortly after starting high school, I started taking flying lessons. I was sixteen and one-half years old. On October 18, 1942, I soloed and then joined the Civil Air Patrol. Due to the war, flying was restricted in Florida and as I wanted to fly (which is why) I joined the CAP. This allowed me to get in some reasonable flying time. ...I remember when the Army Air Force gave us the first military plane, an L-2, which we picked up at Lantana Field near West Palm Beach. I was able to fly from Lantana to Fort Myers in the back seat. At Lantana I was able to see the CAP planes with their bomb racks attached. These planes were used for anti-submarine warfare as well as coastal patrol.*[13]

This young man went on to tell about finding a missing airplane that crashed near Tamiami Trail while on a training mission. A later search for a missing BT-13 from Punta Gorda proved futile but Perry Snell will never forget the opportunity he had to work with the CAP at such a young age.[14] As indicated, some of the CAP planes on the east coast were later equipped to fire at submarines but this was unusual since their jobs were primarily to serve as watchdogs and to keep US forces informed of enemy threats. The airfield in Sarasota became known as the Sarasota-Bradenton International Airport after the war.

Fort Myers also had a CAP unit and was also home to the Page Field Army Air Field where fighter planes and heavy bombers were used by pilots in their training. Russian flight instructors were trained there and many P-59s were sold to the Russians as part of the Lend Lease program. Some of the other fighter aircraft were P-39s, P-40s, P-47s and the famed P-51s. The 98th Bombardment Group dropped 100-pound sand bags on imaginary beach targets during its target practice training while those on the ground fought mosquitoes because of water drainage problems that plagued the area. Fighting and bomber squadrons trained here for about three months and then moved on overseas. Colonel James Doolittle, after training at Eglin, moved here to determine the feasibility of launching B-26 bombers from carrier decks, a practice used on his raids over Japan that made him famous.

The information on military bases listed on these pages is simply an overview of the total package and doesn't attempt to offer readers a comprehensive listing since each branch of the service offered diverse services and personnel that would be impossible to list separately. Indeed, hundreds of pages would likely be required to adequately show the extension to which the military installations permeated the entire peninsula of Florida during the war years. Because of the enormity of the task, there are obviously many omissions.

However, it seems imperative that some additional effort

be made to show just how extensive the military's presence was in the Sunshine State. Therefore, an attempt is designed to do this by highlighting *only one* branch of the service, outlining in detail the extremely large congregate of services offered at locations scattered extensively throughout the state. (Space, quite naturally, would not have allowed this breakdown to be done for each branch of the service.) The US Navy was selected at random to illustrate the enormous presence of the military that saturated Florida during the war years. Regretfully, this will necessitate a bit of repetition since the Navy was already included in the previous overview. This listing, hopefully, will show just how extensive the presence of the military was in Florida. The more detailed locations and activities of the US Navy are as follows:[15]

**Banana River:** Naval Air Station, O-in-C Commissary Store, Air Bomber's Training Unit, NAS (46398), Operational Training Unit VPB2 #3, NAS (46399)

**Bay Pines:** Veterans Administration (46548C)

**Boca Raton:** Army Air Force, Technical Training School

**Boca Chica:** Anti-Submarine Warfare Training Unit, NAAS (46460)

**Brownsville:** Branch Intelligence Office

**Bushnell:** Florida Field Trial Project Program

**Camp Blanding:** Armed Forces Induction Station

**Cecil Field:** Auxiliary Air Station

**Coral Gables:** Navy V-12 Unit, University of Miami School

**Corry Field:** Auxiliary Air Station

**Crescent City:** Naval Air Operational Training Command Auxiliary Boat Facility

**Daytona Beach:** Naval Air Station, Air Operational

Training Base, Daytona Beach Boat Works, Inc.

**Deland:** Naval Air Station, Naval Aviation Operational Training Bases, Naval Rest Center, College Arms Hotel, Fleet Air Detachment

**Dinner Key:** US Naval Air Facility

**Dunedin:** Amphibian Tractor Detachment, Marine Corps, 7th N.D.

**Elgin Field:** Army Air Force Proving Ground Command, Elgin Field (35608A), Headquarters, 1st Proving Ground Torpedo Squad (Composite)

**Ellyson Field:** Auxiliary Air Station

**Flagler Beach:** Coast Guard Beach Patrol Station, No. 5 (39023)

**Fort Lauderdale:** Naval Air Station, Section Base, Inshore Patrol, Naval Aviation Operational Training Base, Naval Ordnance Research Facilities, Inshore Patrol, Section Base, Naval Air Operational Training Command Boat Facility (Port Everglades), Dooley's Basin & Drydock, Inc., US Naval Magazine, Naval Ordnance Unit (45731), Naval Training School (Radar and Director Operators at Lauderdale Beach Hotel), Naval Training School (Fire Control), Coast Guard Patrol Base (Port Everglades), Anti-Submarine Development Detachment, Atlantic Surface Division (Sea Duty)

**Fort Myers:** Assistant Supervisor of Shipbuilding, Fort Myers Shipbuilding Co., Army Air Forces Flexible Gunnery Central Instructors School (49008)

**Fort Pierce:** Naval Amphibious Training Base (A-3226), Naval Air Operational Training Command Boat Facility, Demolition Unit, Amphibious Training Base, Scout & Radar School, Joint Army & Navy Experimental & Testing Board for the Removal of Underwater Obstacles, Branch Intelligence Office (30189), Navy Relief Office, Anti-Aircraft Training Center

**Fort William** (Miami): Harbor Entrance Control Post (13337B)

**Gainesville:** School at University of Florida

**Green Cove Springs:** US Naval Auxiliary Air Station

**Hialeah:** Gibbs Harrison Co. (Inspection Duty Station)

**Hobe Sound:** Southern Signal Corps School at Camp Murphy

**Hollywood:** Three Tactical Radar Training Schools at Hollywood Beach Hotel

**Homestead:** Resident OinC of Construction (at Homestead Air Base)

**Jacksonville:** Chief of Naval Air Operational Training, Air Warning Center, Naval Air Station, Army Market Center, Section Base, Resident OinC of Construction, Merrill Steven Dry Dock and Repair Co., OinC, Clothing & Stores, Aviation Service Schools, Navy Recruiting Station, Hospital, Office of District Intelligence Officer, Assistant District Intelligence Officer, Navy cost Inspector, Gibbs Gas Engine Co., Navy Cost Inspector, Merrill Stevens Dry Dock & Repair Co., Port Director, Naval Transportation Service, Naval Receiving Station, Ship's Store Ashore, Naval Aviation

Operational Training Bases, Naval Air Gunners School, Naval Air Technical Training Center, Armed Forces Induction Station, Malaria Field Training, Florida State Health Department, Air Bombers School, Student Officers' Headquarters, Indoctrination School, Aviation Engineering Officers' School, Naval Advisor to the Branch Office, Army Information Center, Navy Marketing Officer, Epidemiological Unit No. 48, Huckins Yacht Corp. Cost Inspector, etc., etc. (Jacksonville was home to 62 units, including everything from training schools for cooks and bakers to air bombing units.)

**Jupiter:** Naval Radio Direction Finder, Naval Radio Station, Supplementary Radio Station (40732A)

**Key West:** Naval Air Station, Naval Operating Base, Repair Base, US Coast Guard Patrol Base (2963A-1), Fleet Sonar School (49036) Mine Warfare Office, 7th N.D. (33151), etc. (Key West was home to 37 units, including everything from submarine training activity to providing barracks for the Marines.)

**Lake City:** Naval Air Station, Resident OinC of Construction of Contract NOy-5536.

**Lynn Haven:** General American Tank Storage & Terminals Co. and Navy Petroleum Inspector

**Marathon:** Coast Guard Patrol Base

**Mayport:** Naval Air Operational Training Command Boat Facility, Naval Auxiliary Air Station (1847)

**Melbourne:** Naval Air Station, Resident OinC of

Construction of Naval Operational Training Station Contract NOy-5535

**Miami:** Naval Air Station, Captain of the Port, Cable Censor, Coast Guard Station, Commissary Store, Prigg Boat Words, District Intelligence Officer, Resident Intelligence Officer, District Security Office, Destroyer Escort Training Unit, etc., etc. (Miami was home to 60 units, including everything from its naval barracks to regional air traffic coordination.)

**Miami Beach:** Harbor Entrance Signal Station, Navigation Training Unit, NAS, Naval Dispensary (12025)

**Miami Springs:** Inspector of Naval Aircraft, Intercontinental Aircraft Corp., Bureau of Aeronautics Representative Consolidated Vultee Corp., Navy Cost Inspector

**Milton:** Naval Auxiliary Air Station

**Morgan City:** OinC of Construction, Naval Floating Dry Dock

**New Smyrna:** Branch Intelligence Office, Naval Air Operational Training Command Boat Facility

**Opa Locka:** Naval Air Station (often listed as Miami)

**Orlando:** Air Combat Control Squadrons (Amphibious 1 & 2), Army Air Forces Tactical Center, School of Applied Tactics, Army Air Forces Boards

**Palm Beach:** Coast Guard Training Station, Training School for Spars, Naval Convalescent Hospital, Headquarters Caribbean Division, Air Transport Command, 1100th AAF Base Unit at West Palm Beach

## Jim Wiggins

**Panama City:** Captain of the Port, Branch Intelligence Office, Port Director, Assistant Industrial Manager, US Naval Amphibious Training Base at St. Andrews Bay

**Pensacola:** Naval Air Station, Naval Barin Auxiliary Air Station, Naval Air Training Center Bronson Field Auxiliary, Clothing & Small Stores, Naval Hospital, Saufley Field Auxiliary, Whiting Field Auxiliary, Naval Air Training Schools, etc. (Pensacola was home to 26 units, including everything from the Celestial Navigation Training Units to gunnery training schools.)

**Port Everglades:** Naval Air Operational Training Command Boat Facility, Harbor Entrance Signal Station, Port Director, US Coast Guard Patrol Base

**Richmond:** Naval Air Station, Airship Headquarters Squadron Detachment 21, Public Works Department

**Saint Augustine:** US Coast Guard Training Station, Zone Intelligence Office, Naval Liaison Officer, Coast Guard Beach Patrol Station No. 3 at Marineland, Florida Selective Service Center

**Saint Petersburg:** US Maritime Service Training Station, Office of Public Relations, Harbor Entrance Signal Station (Egmont Key), Coast Guard Air Station, War Shipping Administration, Maritime Service Training Station, Coast Guard Air Station (1599) Joint Army-Navy Airplane Repair Boat Base

**Sanford:** Naval Air Station, Naval Aviation Operational

## Jim Wiggins

> Training Base

**Smyrna:** Naval Air Operational Training Command Boat Facility

**Tallahassee:** Branch Intelligence Office

**Tampa:** Captain of the Port, Naval Inspector of Ordnance, Tampa Shipbuilding Corp., Inc. Port Director, Naval Advisor, War Production Board, Bushnell-Lyons Iron Works, Inc., Navy Recruiting Station, Harbor Entrance Signal Station (Egmont Key), OinC of Construction, Procurement Class V-7 Personnel, Naval Receiving Station, Chief of Mine Warfare Mission, Navy Routing Office, Zone Intelligence Office, Supervisor of Shipbuilding, Tampa Shipbuilding Co., Inc.

**Tarpon Springs:** Branch Intelligence Office of District Intelligence Organization

**Vero Beach:** Naval Air Station, Air Operational Base (3293)

**Wakula:** Resident Inspector, Naval Material, Newport Ships

Again, this extensive detailed listing includes *only* the branch of the US Navy and its presence in Florida. Multiply this by all of the other branches of the US military and this will give an indication of just how saturated Florida was with bases and military operations. No area in the Sunshine State was untouched. The war effort was everywhere.

❧ ❧

# Chapter Four

# The War on Florida's East Coast

As noted, the establishment and expansion of military bases in Florida served as a forewarning long before the bombing of Pearl Harbor. People in the US had been constantly warned by President Roosevelt that they could not afford to be apathetic in their views about their own personal involvement in the war. But there still seemed to be an entrenched sense of false security in knowing that they were divided from the rest of the world by the wide oceans of the Atlantic and Pacific. Many felt quite smug in their physical isolation, somewhat like residents of a castle being buttressed by a surrounding moat. However, the fact would soon become apparent that the moat was filled with predators and that the so-called castle could be penetrated anywhere along the US eastern shoreline and, in particular, in Florida's waters which were soon to be teeming with German U-boats.

## Jim Wiggins

Such a huge intrusion would have been thought impossible when, in 1939, the Germans had only 57 U-boats. But Germany's push for power soon included command of the undersea waters as Hitler's threat to the world increased. In September 1939, Karl Doenitz, the German U-boat admiral, had only 30 short-range coastal type submarines and 27 ocean going vessels but by July, 1942, he had 300 and said that he "could strangle Britain to death" because of the pre-war expansion phase that was referred to as the "Z plan."[1]

After the Japanese attack on Pearl Harbor, German Admiral Doenitz studied the situation carefully and decided that one of the most vulnerable areas for his enemies was located right under their noses, an area that had a stream of ships lined up like sitting ducks on the East Coast of the United States and in the Gulf of Mexico. Merchant ships coming and going from Texas, Louisiana, Venezuela, the Dutch West Indies and other areas in Central and South America while en route to New York and New Jersey were hauling fuel and other products necessary for the operation and support of war needs. Being a peninsula, Florida's coastlines were particularly vulnerable. Not only would the sinking of ships prove beneficial in terms of destroying needed supplies, particularly crude oil, gasoline, and petroleum derivatives, but also there was bound to be an emotional impact upon a citizenry that could actually look out and view a war going on right before their eyes. The psychological impact upon US morale could be utterly disastrous. Floridians, in particular, would soon be in shock and could not believe what was happening in their own backyard.

Historian Michael Gannon, one of the world's leading authorities on the subject of U-boats, stressed the importance placed by the Germans upon swiftness and the use of surprise in the initial attacks in US waters. Herein let it be noted that Professor Gannon's books offer a thorough and unique analyses of the entire U-boat operation, particularly because his perspective includes first-hand observations derived from interviews and detailed reports after the war offered by men such as Reinhard Hardegen, captain of the famed German submarine, U-123 and other German crewmen who took part in the encounters. Thus, Gannon's analysis of the U-boat activity is personalized and documented in such a way that makes the reader cognizant of underlying plans and augmentation that could not have been available to the public, offering invaluable details that would have otherwise been lost. In his book, *Operation Drumbeat*, he writes:

> ***Paukenschlag*** *was designed to inflict a sudden severe injury on the American enemy. The blow would come like a thunderbolt...or like the percussion of a timpani stick on the tightly stretched head of a brass-barreled drum. Intended were quick, violent sinkings and resounding psychological shock.*[2]

Gannon later augmented his earlier observations in his comprehensive book on activity in the Atlantic, *Black May*, with the suggestion that "What was meant here was not 'drumroll,' as some would have it," but, rather, a 'sudden blow'" that would come with simultaneous attacks on the same day.[3] Everything would be quick and decisive, an important element in the ingenious planning by Admirable Doenitz.

Admiral Doenitz recommended that one dozen U-boats be sent immediately to the Atlantic Seaboard area of the US. Thankfully, the German High Command approved only six types 1X U-boats to be deployed to the United States waters. One of those submarines, the U-128, was in repair and unable to meet the deadline for departure. The operation was called *Paukenschlag*, the German word for drumbeat. Thereafter, *Operation Drumbeat* became synonymous with mass destruction by German U-boats that would initially sink 238 ships in the first nine months of 1942, an astronomical number that is hard to imagine. But for Floridians, the sinking of ships in their own waters by the Nazis would soon become all too real.

The first of the five German U-boats, U-125 (Folkers), left Europe on December 18, 1941. It was followed by U-123 (Hardegen) on the 23rd and U-66 (Za) on the 24th. U-130 (Kals) and U-119 (Bleichrodt) sailed three days later. They arrived in US waters a little over two weeks later and the plan was for the operation to begin on Jan. 13. There were orders not to strike any outbound cruise ships but other targets such as cruisers, carriers, or battleships would be readily acceptable prizes.

Comments about the presence of the German U-boats in US waters is aptly described by the historian, David Kahn:

> *The entry of the United States into the war against Germany on December 11, 1941, voided Hitler's concerns about sinking American vessels, and Doenitz sent his U-boats to the rich hunting grounds off the East Coast. Here freighters and tankers, trawlers and barges, marched individually up and down the coast, disbanding the lessons of convoy so painfully learned by the British over two world wars. And they did so before a blaze of city lights, foolishly kept burning by chambers of commerce afraid of loosing business during tourist season. As a consequence, for six months the U-boats enjoyed what they called 'happy time,' sinking dozens of ships, sometimes within sights of crowds on shore, with barely a loss of their own.*[4]

The first strike did not wait until the agreed upon date but, rather, was moved up two days when the *SS Cycops* moved into the sights of the U-123 as an easy target. The opportunity offered was simply too tempting. This was followed with the sinking of two other ships within two days by U-130. They were easy pickings and Admiral Donitz was elated that his plans for surprise attacks were being augmented better than had been expected. This was the beginning of a nightmare along the US Seaboard at a time when Americans were ill prepared for war. The so-called "happy time" was under way in northern US waters and there was absolutely nothing that could be done about it.

One of the great debates about the tragedy inflicted upon Allied shipping lanes in US waters centered around Admiral Ernest J. King, Commander in Chief of the US Atlantic Fleet The German U-boats were tracked all the way from France and Admiral King pulled all of his destroyers home, stating, "The immediate probability of submarine attack in that area, and the weakness of our coastal defense force, make it essential that the maximum practicable number of our destroyers be based at home bases."[5]

The US Navy Department continued to track the enemy submarines into American waters but the 21 US destroyers foolishly remained docked at stations from Maine to Virginia. No ships were deployed nor was there any declaration of a pending emergency. Instead, all of Admiral King's ships were held in port or were shipped out for other missions while German U-boats lurked in the waters off New York Harbor and elsewhere along the Eastern Seaboard. U-boats lay silent on the bottom during the day but Gannon describes the night scene "like Prussian deer hunters in camp chairs waiting for game to be driven in front of their guns."[6] Gannon also stated that the attacks were referred to by the Germans as the "Great American Turkey Shoot."[7]

It was one of the most frustrating and frightening times in US history as an average of at least one allied ship per day was sunk by German U-boats attacking as far south as Cape Hatteras. The sinkings were employed as great propaganda tools and it was obviously apparent that Hitler's regime was thoroughly enjoying the game of cat and mouse, knowing full well that they were acting with impunity. (Rather, the activity was much more vigorous than any cat chasing after its prey. An honest analogy would be more like that which takes place in a shooting gallery where the targets were all lined up in a row.)

The first wave of attacks left 25 ships sunk, which totaled out to nearly 157,000 tons and had more than surpassed Germany's plan to make the surprise attacks fast and brutal. One U-boat, the Hardegen (U-123), alone sank nine ships for a total of 53,173 tons. The five "Drumbeaters" left the US Eastern Seaboard on February 6 for their ports in France. The quick surprise attacks of this initial operation known as *Paukenschlag* was over but this was just the beginning of the carnal display in US waters that was to follow. Other U-boats were waiting in the depths to be deployed in massive attacks of tyranny much greater than could have been imagined.

Historians agree that the impact by German U-boat attacks in the early stages of the war cannot be exaggerated. Over 397 ships were sunk by German submarines within the first six months after the declaration of war. Twice as many people died at the hands of enemy submarines than were killed in the attack on Pearl Harbor on December 7. The negative impact on American morale was tremendous and the German strategy to attack in the narrow shipping lanes off the US Eastern coast proved to be one of the most highly successful German strategies in the entire war. Indeed, *Operation Drumbeat* was a major blow to American security but also fostered a sense of urgency and growing patriotic endeavors that would serve as an impetus for strengthening US power at all levels. The sinkings were likened by many as bully attacks on defenseless children.

Technically, *Paukenschlag* was over in the first wave of attacks by the five German submarines that ended on February 6. The operation had been designed to be surprising, quick, decisive and, for all purposes, that mission had been accomplished. But now there would be new waves of U-boats launched from

European shores that were commanded by experienced captains which Admiral Doenitz did not refer to as the *Paukenschlag* but, rather, as an entirely different operation.

However, for all purposes, and particularly for war historians, the additional waves of attacks were most often viewed as an extension of *Operation Drumbeat*. American Allies, in particular, would find it hard to separate the initial destruction wrought in January and February of 1942 with those that came in the following months. The two appeared inseparable and later operations were but a mere extension of the same mission by Germany to wreck havoc on allied shipping lines. For that reason they have been generally referred to continually by the same German name *Paukenschlag* or its English designation *Operation Drumbeat*.

The Hardegen (U-123) would be among those returning because of its excellent record in the first offensive and vessels such as the U-552 (Topp) the U-129 (Witt), and the U-160 (Lassen) would join with a host of other submarines to continue their plague on the US eastern shoreline. As indicated, *Operation Drumbeat* was technically over but the activity of U-boats in US waters was just beginning and the shipping lanes of Florida waters were destined to become prey to these silent sharks, which lurked just below its surface.

The captain of the same submarine (U-128) that destroyed the *Pan Massachusetts* was soon to reap another harvest with the sinking of Cities Service *Empire* off the coast of Melbourne on February 22 just before daybreak. It was hauling 4 million gallons of crude oil from Texas while en route to Philadelphia. Miraculously, 36 of the 50 men on board survived and were picked up by a Navy destroyer and Coast Guard patrol boat. The dead and wounded were unloaded at Fort Pierce.

The same evening of February 22 also witnessed the sinking of the *W.D. Anderson* with its load of crude oil just twelve miles north of Jupiter. Eliot Kleinberg, a staff member of the *Palm Beach Post,* shares a story about a young man's escape from the inferno on his first trip to Florida. His name was Frank Leonard Terry who was 22 years of age at the time when the torpedo struck. Coated in oil, he bobbled in the water for three hours before being rescued. His comments about the ordeal were as follows, "It was my first trip to Florida. I didn't like the experience. When I finally thought of my pals, they were in my prayers. I was a nervous wreck. The Germans? I figure it was war. It was their duty."[8]

After February there seemed to be a lull in operations as allied leadership tried to evaluate the damage done in such a short period of time, restricting their shipping for a time because of the enormous pressure of dealing with the constant surveillance by enemy U-boats. Too, the lull gave ample time for the German submarines to regroup and refuel at their "Milkcows" waiting in the Caribbean, at the same time taking extra precautionary measures to elude detection by the few US units capable of intervention.

What, then, could the US do as a stopgap during this crucial time when production of military apparatus was still being built? What temporary measures could be taken by the Coast Guard and Navy? How could the limited US air power be strengthened? No one could deny that something needed to be done. Deterrents were absolutely necessary but the means to respond with urgency were limited despite the intensity of attacks, which were steadily growing. Few options were available.

## Jim Wiggins

The US Navy immediately established the North Atlantic Coastal Frontier when it became apparent that America's shorelines were at risk. The Frontier was under the command of Rear Admiral Adolhus Andrews and was destined to absorb the Southern 6th Naval District, which reached down into northern Florida waters. The Gulf Sea Frontier was born on February 6, 1942, with commands established in the Caribbean, the Gulf of Mexico and designed to protect the waters from Jacksonville to

Photo 16 - Lookout towers like this one on Hutchinson Island were distributed all along the Atlantic and Gulf coastlines to watch for German submarines or enemy aircraft. (*Florida Archives*)

Texas from the German submarine menace. But none of these commands had the resources to prevent or strike back at the offensive audacity of German U-boats.

Floridians, in particular, sought ways to express their concern and patriotic duty. Teenagers and others were recruited to man watch towers set up at intervals every three miles or so along the eastern shoreline between Jacksonville and Miami and on others that were scattered along the beaches of Gulf waters. Watchers were instructed to rush to a telephone when aircraft was

## Jim Wiggins

spotted and report with the words "Army-Flash," a code that would prompt the operator to contact the appropriate military personnel.[9]

On May 23, 1941, Admiral King ordered that small civilian boats could be utilized for shore patrols, a move readily endorsed by organizations of Florida yachtsmen and commercial fishermen of Florida who cooperated fully with the program. It was called the Corsair Navy but was commonly referred to as the "Mosquito Fleet" or "Hooligan's Navy." An auxiliary of the Coast Guard originally took over this operation but eventually the Coast Guard became totally responsible for this unit, which recruited seaworthy boats that were 50 to 100 feet in length. The assistance given to survivors of sunken ships proved to be invaluable and offered a bit of temporary relief in the absence of US military sea craft. The Corsair Navy was comprised of a rather motley assortment of vessels and untrained leadership but was seaworthy and adequate enough to offer temporary relief to the problems facing ships in Florida's troubled waters. After all, *any* craft was better than none and Florida's citizens were anxious to do whatever they could to help.

Residents, particularly teenagers, were even drafted to ride horses for patrol along Florida's Atlantic beaches and dog patrols paraded up and down to sniff out any suspicious activity. One must remember that back in the 1940s the beaches usually swarmed with pesky mosquitoes and sand fleas (no seeums). Thus, the hardships on volunteers were quite severe, particularly during the warm summer months. But willing recruits were always readily available to do their bit for the war cause.

The Civil Air Patrol was first set up at Morrison Field in West Palm Beach but was extended to include units all across Florida. Admiral King even authorized some of the planes of the Civil Air Control to be armed. Civilians were ready and eager to go forward in the service of their country and every means

## Jim Wiggins

possible was soon being used to enhance US strength against the enemies knocking on the front door of Florida's shoreline. However, communities along the coastline were often reticent in the beginning to cooperate with the request for complete blackouts, fearing that this might jeopardize the tourists industry that continued to grow at a rapid pace in spite of the war.

As already noted, the Navy, meanwhile, established a plan to use slow-moving blimps as a means of detecting U-boats in Florida's waters. Blimp bases were located at Key West, Homestead and north on the Banana River. The Naval Air Station Richmond was the US blimp base that was situated on more than two thousand acres in the area where the Miami Zoo is located today. The base opened on September 15, 1942, toward the end of the most active era of U-boats movement in Florida waters and helped signal the fact that the US was no longer willing to accept the enemy's presence in nearby shipping lanes. There were three, 17-story hangars that surrounded a huge circular concrete pad.

The presence of blimps floating overhead became a great deterrent for U-boat operations. The psychological impact of having someone looking over one's shoulders was far more beneficial, however, than the actual threat to the operations of the submarines. Only one blimp, the K-74, was shot down by enemy fire from U-boats. K-74 was hit in July of 1942 by small arms fire just south of Miami and slowly deflated as the U-boat quickly submerged and disappeared. The 10-man crew was rescued by a nearby US destroyer.

After a brief interlude of several months, the *Gulf State*, a tanker carrying crude oil from Corpus Christi to Portland, was sunk on April 3 by two torpedoes off Key West. Thirty lives were lost.

The *SS Gulfamerica* was on its first and last voyage off Jacksonville on April 10th when it was sighted by the German U-boat, U-123, under the command of Lieutenant Richard Hardegen.

The story of this sinking is one of the most interesting for history buffs. Historian Gannon met with the German captain after the war and was told that he wanted to conserve torpedoes but knew that the slain ship's hull had to be ventilated in order to make it sink. However, he saw people standing on the beach and didn't want to harm them so he maneuvered his submarine into position so that he was between the beach and the burning ship. It was only then that he used his deck gun to finish off the job. Gannon reports on the scene:

> *Not satisfied that the tanker with its compartmentation would sink when its cargo burned out, Hardegen ordered the deck guns manned and approached the broken vessel with the intent of holing her fatally with artillery. When he saw the large number of spectators on shore, however, and noted the proximity of the beach homes to the point of attack, he worried that the shells he fired from seaward might overshoot and hurt innocent people and their property. He therefore made a turn around the victim's stern and came up on its shoreward, or port side, where any errant shells would pass harmlessly out to sea.*[10]

Hardegen later wrote: "All the vacationers had seen an impressive special performance at Roosevelt's expense. A burning tanker, artillery fire, the silhouette of a U-boat ... how often had all of that been seen in America."[11]

An article written by Terry Tomalin in the *St. Petersburg Times* quotes Phil May who was on the Jacksonville boardwalk at the time. May recalls:

## Jim Wiggins

*I was 17 and on a double date with a friend of mine. We were on the merry-go-round and when we came around to face the ocean, there was just this tremendous explosion and ball of fire shooting straight up in the air. We didn't think that it could possibly have anything to do with the war, but as we drove north; we stopped and watched as the German submarine came between the beach and the burning ship and finished it off with its deck gun.*[12]

Photo 17 - A tanker is ablaze off Jupiter Inlet after being hit by a German submarine. *(Florida Archives)*

May continued:

"*He was probably no more than a mile off the beach. We could see the outline of the submarine clearly. And each time the deck gun went off, the whole thing lit up.*"[13]

Miraculously, 29 of the 38 men survived and were taken to Mayport near Jacksonville. Two days later the *Leslie*, hauling

## Jim Wiggins

300 tons of sugar from Cuba to New York, was sunk off Cape Canaveral. All but four of the 32 men survived. A day later the *Korsholm*, a freighter loaded with nearly 5,000 tons of phosphate, was sunk nearby with the loss of nine lives out of 26 crewmen.

The month of April was filled with chaos but the month of May was even worse. The first three days of the month saw four ships attacked with the loss of many lives. The four ships were the *La Paz*, the *Ocean Venus*, the *Laertes*, a freighter carrying over 5,000 tons of military supplies; and, the *Sami*. These attacks all took place in the waters off Cape Canaveral and Melbourne.

The British tanker, the *Eclipse*, loaded down with fuel for aircraft, was offshore a short distance from Boynton Beach shortly after midnight on May 4th when it received a surprise attack from the direction of the beach. The German U-564 had managed to boldly wedge itself between the vessel and shore to avoid having its silhouette seen against a full moon. Two men were killed, 29 escaped in lifeboats to Boynton Inlet, and 16 remained with the ship, which was later towed to Port Everglades in Fort Lauderdale for repair.

The freighter, *De Lislie*, was also damaged off Boynton Beach, followed by an attack the next day of the *Java Arrow* off Fort Pierce. The Dutch freighter, the *Amazone*, loaded with 900 tons of coffee and other products, was sunk off Fort Pierce. The U-333 then claimed its third kill within five hours by sinking the 7,000-ton oil tanker, the *Halsey*, off Jupiter Island. The survivors were taken to Gilbert's Bar House of Refuge on Hutchinson Island. On May 8th the *Ohion* was sunk during daylight hours off Boca Raton with 6,000 tons of ore, 1,300 tons of licorice root and 300 tons of wool. Fifteeen men were lost and the 17 survivors were taken to West Palm Beach. The *Lubrafol*, sailing from Aruba to New York with fuel oil, was sunk off Delray Beach the next day.

Imagine, if you will, what an impact these sinkings had upon the residents of Florida's east coast. Burning ships, survivors arriving on shore in lifeboats, dead washing ashore and the constant threat of war right in the front yard of residents who were already enduring the reality of having their loved ones and friends shipped off to fight a war in some faraway land; it must have been a very stressful experience for everyone. Talk about reality! This was, indeed, the reality show of all reality shows.

Admiral Doenitz and Admiral Raeder were elated over the success of their operations and asked for a meeting with Hitler on March 12 of 1942. They stressed the importance for Germany's need to take advantage of the "unpreparedness of the United

Photo 18 - The tanker, Gulfland, burns a short distance off Hobe Sound after being torpedoed by a German submarine. *(Florida Archives)*

States" and outlined their plan to further strengthen the Nazi's resolve to continue and strengthen their U-boat destruction on merchant ships with major expansion into the waters of the Gulf.[14]

Perhaps it should be pointed out that some German military leaders were critical of the U-boat operations because they were not sinking ships en route from America to Britain. Admiral Doenitz, however, supported his operations by pointing out that the same objectives were being met and that it did not really matter where ships were sunk since all of them were carrying cargoes necessary for support of the war. Whether they were sunk in the North Atlantic or off the shoreline of Florida was inconsequential. Rather, he contended that there was one unified shipping network and that the ultimate objective was a "race between sinking and new construction."[15] German leadership reasoned that the materials on each sunken ship had to be replaced no matter where it was destroyed and each fatality meant a delay of materials available for Allied use, thus contributing to America's unpreparedness for war.

Both Doenitz and Admiral Raeder recognized the fact that the time would come when they would no longer be allowed to operate with impunity and that the sinking of their submarines would prove too costly in the future. Raeder declared at the Fuehrer conference in May of 1942 that "if operations in America should prove unprofitable, we shall resume warfare against the convoys in the North Atlantic with a large number of U-boats."[16] But both admirals were unimpressed with the US increased attempts to thwart their efforts. They referred to US naval and air operations as having "inexperienced crews which do not constitute a serious threat at present." Admiral Raeder even suggested that "American fliers see nothing, the destroyers and patrol vessels are traveling too fast most of the time even to locate submarines, or they are not persistent enough in their pursuit with depth charges."[17] Though they acknowledged the incompetence of US resistance, they knew all too well that the time would soon come when their presence in American waters would be limited.

Hundreds of people along the east coast of Florida witnessed the sinking of ships by enemy submarines. The experience was not second-handed but, rather, was a live first-hand experience that brought the reality of the war home to Floridians long before most of the citizenry of the United States had adapted to the fact that our nation was really at war. Watching a burning ship offshore was not only shocking but elicited emotions never felt before by Americans who had never witnessed any kind of war activity on their own soil. The stories about those days in 1942 are numerous.

In her book, *My Gold Coast*, author Lora Sinks Britt, relates how three rescues were carried out from the Delray Beach/Boynton area within one week. One was a British tanker that was grounded on a reef when trying to evade a German U-boat; the other was an American merchant ship sunk after being torpedoed; and the other was an allied ship that left its crew bobbing in oil-slick waters. She writes:

Ruby Coompte was gathering shells on the beach near the foot of Vista del Mar Drive when she saw the torpedoing of the merchant ship. She ran to the W.J. Enright home across the boulevard and breathlessly reported what she had just witnessed. The word was relayed to the defense units by telephone, and soon rescue boats were on the way. The ship's crew was prepared for the emergency, which the captain had feared would arise; they had lashed oil drums together to form rafts, knowing that there might not even be time to lower the life boats if they became a target for a German submarine. Twenty-two men were saved by the drums but 15 others lost their lives.[18]

Another account shared by author Britt are the recollections of Louisa A. Robins (Mrs. Thomas Robins) who tells of being on a boat with its owners, Bill and Emily Kebb, along with her husband and daughter. Their daughter, Mary, looked out over the water and shouted, "Look, that ship's been torpedoed!" Mary Robins and Emily Kebb jumped overboard to make more room for survivors while Louisa joined with her husband, Tom, and Bill to help in the rescue as the boat was turned seaward to the wreck that was eight miles offshore.

## Jim Wiggins

*We skirted this terrible flotsam, searching for human life,' said Louisa. 'There were so many black things all over that at first it was difficult to pick out anything. Then what appeared to be a floating timber started to swim in the center of the silent, catastrophic mess. Gradually, some of the black spots became little clumps of men strewn amidst the debris. Tom threw out a lifeline to three men huddled motionless on something as Bill maneuvers the* Furious *around the debris. This human flotsam climbed into the little boat. Seaman Edward Reville had great difficulty because his arm was broken. Next came a life raft with four motionless men aboard bobbing about in the waves. They pointed to a colorless lump of wreckage. 'Get that man over there, first,' shouted one. 'He's the captain and he can't swim a stroke. He's almost gone. We can wait.' The captain was clinging to an old piece of gangway. He was on his stomach with his face almost in the water. Bill had to leave the helm to help in getting the captain aboard. His hands were numb and tangled in the rungs of the piece of old gangway to which he was clinging; they were cut and blistered.*[19]

The captain had been at the bottom of his boat, the *S.S. Ohioan,* when it was hit but managed to find his way to the surface when the ship listed. Bill's boat *Furious* rescued nine men and two other boats picked up a dozen men. Two were taken aboard dead and 16 men remained lost. The captain said that they were likely killed by steam from the exploding boilers when the ship was struck. The ship had left Bombay, India, on the day that war was declared and would have soon been home after traveling over 28,000 miles before being sunk. Who would have believed that it happened off the beaches of Florida's east coast!

Britt also shared the humorous story told of Third

## Jim Wiggins

Engineer David Graham who said that he had always wanted to visit Palm Beach "but I sure never expected to come in such a costume."[20] He had been asleep in his bunk when the torpedo struck and found himself floating completely naked when help arrived. He was embarrassed and held his life preserver in front to hide his nakedness.

Floridians along the Atlantic never expected to see war activity on the home front but 98 ships were sunk between May through July on the sand frontier which reached from Jacksonville to Cuba. *Operation Drumbeat* had already included the sinking of 82 merchant ships along the eastern seaboard between Boston and Jacksonville in the months between January through April and all of these sinkings added up to a very stressful situation with such a barrage of carnage that would have earlier been deemed completely unlikely by everyone.

# Jim Wiggins

# Chapter Five

# U-Boats in the Gulf

At 12 years of age I remember going with my older cousin, Kline Condo, to climb the lookout tower, which was recently erected on the beach near the end of Pine Avenue at Anna Maria Island on the Gulf of Mexico. It was the summer of 1942. I was visiting for a couple of days at their beach cottage which was less than a block away and Kline was a patrol volunteer, serving duty two nights a week on the tower. Word had it that German enemy submarines were in the Gulf waters and sightings needed to be reported.

Porpoises at play did not count. Nor did the occasional turtle crawling up in the tidewater to lay its eggs. Were enemy airplanes also in the area? Likely not. But the news of Pearl Harbor's attack made anything seem possible. Blackout curtains were ordered to be in place and shore patrols walked the beaches to make sure that the orders were followed. Unlike communities on the Atlantic, which were reluctant in the early months to prohibit lights dimmed along the shoreline because of the fear of losing tourists, members of the Gulf communities immediately responded with blackouts when first learning that ships were being attacked offshore.

Floridians on the west coast of Florida were very much aware of the activity by German U-boats in the waters of the Atlantic only months before. Stories of the sinkings close offshore in such familiar places as Jacksonville, Fort Pierce, Jupiter, West Palm, Boca Raton, Fort Lauderdale, Miami and numerous other spots along the Atlantic Seaboard were, indeed, unbelievably shocking. No one would have ever thought that the Germans would be so brazen as to bring their acts of terror to Florida waters. But for most residents of Florida's west coast, the war was still somewhat distant since no vessels of destruction had entered the Gulf of Mexico, the great placid basin of water that was like their own backyard swimming pool. In fact, the entrance into the Gulf had been limited to the Straits of Florida and the Yucatan channels, adding a bit of security somewhat like those living within a gated community with only one entrance. The feeling was that the Germans would not dare to move into the limited space of the Gulf waters. But that was to change. No longer would merchant vessels in the Gulf of Mexico be immune to the ravages of enemy torpedoes. Fifty-eight ships would soon be sunk in the Gulf between the months of May through September of 1942. This would amount to the sizable amount of over 300,000 tons that would be sent to the bottom.

The invasion into the Gulf of Mexico by German U-boats began on May 4, 1942, when the 2,686-ton freighter *Norlindo* was sunk just west-northwest of Key West. The attack submarine, U-507, was one of two submarines that had made its way through the Straits of Florida. These two were soon followed by more than one dozen others who were to wreak havoc in the Gulf. Survivors of the *Norlindo* in lifeboats said that they were amazed that the submarine pulled up alongside and offered them forty packs of cigarettes and a cake with French writings on its wrappings.[1]

The sinking of the *Norlinda* would initiate a killing spree in the Gulf that would ultimately witness the sinking of 58 allied vessels and 300,000 tons within a period of six months. Historian Allen Cronenberg suggests some of the factors, which influenced the operations in the Gulf:

> *Three developments during this period influenced the war in the Gulf: the introduction of the type XIV submarine tanker, the entry of Mexico into the war, and the embryonic introduction of the convoy system. Submarine tankers, or "milch cows" made it possible for U-boats to operate for longer periods and thus in more remote areas such as the Gulf of Mexico, the Caribbean, the South Atlantic, and eventually around the Cape of Good Hope in the western Indian Ocean. Refueling could extend the operation of a U-boat by a couple of weeks. The larger Type IX U-boats that generally were operating in the Gulf of Mexico could take up their stations off New Orleans, Galveston, or even Tampico and Vera Cruz and remain there until they had expended their complement of torpedoes and ammunition.*[2]

The sinking of Mexican vessels by German U-boats, the *Potrero del Llano* off Miami in May and the *Faja de Oro* in the Straits of Florida a week later, combined with other episodes which ultimately led to Mexico's proclamation on June 1, 1942, that it was at war with Germany. The Mexican government immediately announced that it would speed up its production of 25 torpedo patrol boats that was already under way. The addition of Mexico as an ally would help facilitate cooperative defenses in the Gulf.

Sinkings in the shipping lanes of the Gulf would rapidly

increase in the summer months as U-boats swarmed like piranhas in the warm bathtub waters with little resistance. Within 12 hours after the first sinking, two more ships, the *Munger T. Ball* and the *Joseph M. Cudahy,* were sunk. The first one exploded immediately upon being hit and the other tried in vain for a period of time to zigzag in the night, but to no avail. The inevitable happened. After these sinkings, an alert was sent out by the US shore station to all ships in the Gulf waters, urging them to shut down all lights.

The German U-boats, including the U-506 and the U-507, made their planned rendezvous south southeast of New Orleans. Two additional freighters were sunk there on May 6 and 7 and on May 8 the Norwegian freighter, the *Tory*, was torpedoed while steaming toward the mouth of the Mississippi. The *Aurora* was also sunk there by Commander Wudemann's U-506.

Interestingly, there was little awareness by Floridians or anyone else that the war had moved so close and with such intensity into Gulf waters. After all, it was not something that the US wanted to overly publicize because of the emotional impact that it would likely elicit from fearful residents. Deep sea fishermen were still doing their thing and normal shipping continued at port cities such as Mobile, Galveston, Pensacola, and Tampa. In fact, employment at these ports was high and shipping remained active. The Pinto Island shipyard in Mobile christened *Arthur Middleton*, its fourth ship and the second one completed within 10 days. Another firm, Gulf Shipbuilding, was completing work on the *USS Capps*, the first destroyer built in the eastern Gulf and the first warship built in Alabama since the Civil War.

On Sunday, May 10, 1942, the *Press Register* of Mobile released the first report about the war activity in the Gulf with headlines screaming about boats being torpedoed by German submarines. The article tried erroneously to link the attacks to masterminding by Baron Edgar von Spiegel, a World War I

## Jim Wiggins

veteran and former German consul in New Orleans. Though unfounded, Americans began to believe that the US was crawling with Nazi spies, encouraged perhaps by the prevalence of posters being circulated such as "Zip Your Lip" and anti-espionage classes sponsored by J. Edgar Hoover's G-Men.

As a child, I recall that my friends and I quite enjoyed the idea of living in a world with spies lurking about. We played G-Men games, enhanced with many myths and childlike imagination, pretending that Germans were lurking in the shadows. Our anti-German indoctrination likely began way back with Hitler's emerging reign of terror in Europe.

However, there was never any proof offered to confirm acts of espionage by local residents who were accused of assisting U-boats in the Gulf. A German accent simply did not suffice to convict loyal American citizens even though they might be under suspicion. Rather, submarine-commanders such as Wurdemann, Schacht, Muller-Stockheim and others were certainly capable enough to employ their own devices to insure success at a time when there was little resistance by the United States. Indeed, they almost had free rein to wreak havoc as they pleased.

After their rendezvous near the mouth of the Mississippi, submarines U-506 and U-507, in particular, enjoyed great success with their attacks on merchant ships. Between May 10 and 20, ten ships were sunk. Commander Schacht's U-507 would have had more sinkings but his torpedoes often malfunctioned. There was limited US air cover, no convoys and only the occasional PT boats, which, for the most part, were ineffective. There was simply no way to impede or restrict the freedom of the U-boats during the early stages of their presence in the Gulf. During late May and early June, four other submarines, Winter's U-103, von Mannstein's U-753, Rasch's U-106 and Rostin's U-158 entered the Gulf to rack up additional strikes. At least 10 German submarines ultimately ended up in the Gulf at the same time and each continued in their attacks with impunity.

    The *St. Petersburg Times* published the following headlines on July 19: SHIP TOLL PASSES 400-MARK, the estimated number of ships sunk in the Atlantic, Caribbean and Gulf waters surrounding Florida.[3] Indeed, on the same morning while residents read this story, another ship, the *Baja California*, a Honduran steam merchant ship, was sunk in the Gulf off Rebecca Shoals by the U-84 while en route from New Orleans to Guatemala. (This ship was carrying several tons of glassware and remains as a prime spot for divers today off the coast of Mexico.)

    Survivors of the *Baja California* were picked up by the Cuban fishing schooner *San Ignacio* and taken to the Havana Naval Station. A differing account says that a daring seaplane pilot picked up 21 of the survivors and crowded them into his nine-passenger plane. These stories illustrate how an abundance of rumors became mixed with actual facts as residents became anxious over the existence of the enemy in their midst. Rumors on both Florida coasts abounded, including similar reports of crewmen visiting local Florida sites, purchasing supplies and even attending movies. (I personally recall how it was reported that some German men came ashore on the island of Anna Maria when we lived there during the summer and went to a local grocery store to purchase drinks and other goods. Of course, many friends were sure that they had seen them and that the stories were true but all such sightings were labeled as mere fantasy by local military investigations.) It is quite understandable how facts often became intertwined with fiction since reality at that time carried mixed messages that were emotionally charged.

    But the tragedy of constant sinkings by German U-boats in Gulf waters was no fantasy. They increased at a rapid pace. Take, for example, the sinking of the *William C. McTarnahan*, one of the 41 ships sunk in the month of May. A story written by C.J. Christ tells the story of three grown sons and their father who were on shrimp trawlers in the Gulf when they spotted a German U-boat not far from their three boats. They were relieved when the submarine moved away. While anchoring for the night they heard an explosion. Christ writes:

> *The victim was the National Bulk Carriers ship, Motor/Tanker William C McTarnahan. She was on a course of 263 degrees, speed 11 knots, four lookouts, completely blacked out, no moonlight, not zigzagging and radio silent. Her position was 35 miles east of Ship Shoal Light, just south of Last Island, Louisiana. The Chief officer had just come on watch at 0400 when he saw two torpedo tracks headed for the ship off the starboard bow. He only had time to shout "hard right" to the quartermaster at the helm, but it was too late. One torpedo struck the #2 cargo tank and the other hit the main engine room and the steering engine room.*[4]

The fishing boats of the Versagi fleet, the *Pioneer, Defender,* and the *Venture,* belonged to the three sons and their father and proceeded to rescue 29 of the crew of 43. One of the badly burned men was put on a bunk but died four hours later. Ira Pete, one of the sons, said later "I gave him a whole bottle of aspirins, 100 in all, but he was burned so badly...that's all we had. (Could the poor soul survive 100 aspirins?) We scrubbed, cleaned and painted the boat, but the smell stayed. It never went away. I never went on board that boat again."[5]

Two days later the Coast Guard officer who had assisted in the transfer of survivors to the Houma and New Orleans hospitals, asked Ira Pete to raise his right hand and put his other hand on a book. Ira Pete was then told that he was now a member of the US Coast Guard. Many stories like this one came out of the sinking and rescue missions as an increasing number of residents who lived on the shorelines of the Gulf became involved while actually witnessing survivors and debris arriving on shore. It was not at all uncommon for residents to discover bodies washed up on the beaches, immersing citizens immediately in the traumatic

Photo 19 - A shrimp boat moves close to rescue survivors from a sinking freighter in the Gulf of Mexico. (*Florida Archives*)

reality of war in their midst.

Between July 7 and July 21 there were at least seven German U-boats active at war in the Gulf of Mexico and were responsible for the sinking of 28 vessels. One submarine, the U-67 under the command of Muller Stockheim, specialized in shallow water operations and cruised from the waters off Appalachicola to the Tortugas and the mouth of the Mississippi, while sinking seven vessels alone. U-158 sank nearly 38,000 tons and U-120 sank over 20,000 tons. (The degree of success was often measured in

## Jim Wiggins

terms of the weight of the merchandise destroyed.) Such success in the Gulf was even greater than what was anticipated earlier by the German commanders.

The story of the *Robert E. Lee*, which was attacked on July 30, 1942, is particularly interesting. This ship was loaded with 270 passengers, many of whom were survivors from ships recently sunk, and was returning to the port of New Orleans from Trinidad. It had been a horrible trip for the passengers who were crowded together with little water, no air conditioning and squalid conditions due to the unavailability of adequate staff and crowded facilities. The complaints were numerous so the ship's captain decided to stop at Tampa to allow passengers to disembark for a while.

Upon arrival off the Egmont Key station at the entrance to Tampa Bay, there was no pilot boat available to take the ship into port. The captain sent a Morse code message by light to their escorting vessel, PC566, asking if they could continue escorting them to New Orleans. Unfortunately, the PC566 then broke radio silence by asking the Gulf Sea Frontier headquarters for permission. German U-boats, in particular the U-166, monitored the request and knew exactly the location of the *Robert E. Lee* and its plans to continue on to New Orleans. At 4:30 p.m. the ship was torpedoed and sank within minutes.

Those aboard the craft witnessed an unusual thing. They saw the torpedo racing along the starboard side of the ship and debated whether the object was a porpoise or shark. It suddenly turned sharply a full 90 degrees and struck the ship just aft of the engine room. Fortunately, most of the 407 persons on board survived because of the quick action by the PC566 and SC519, their escorts and by the tug *Underwriter*, which was waiting nearby to aid in the rescue. Only 15 passengers and 10 crewmembers were lost.

The enemy submarine, U-166, had been laying mines off

the mouth of the Mississippi River and was responsible for the attack and sinking of the *Robert E. Lee*. The US PC566 raced to the scene and dropped depth charges where they had last seen the enemy periscope. An oil slick appeared. Two days late a US Grumman J4F seaplane spotted what they thought was the same submarine and attacked. The two aviators, Henry White and George Boss, were told that it was likely the same U-166 but the event was classified and the pilots were ordered to keep quiet about the sinking.

But much confusion about the identification of the vessel continued. Interestingly, the area where the U-166 was supposedly sunk by the aircraft was much too far away and no remains were ever uncovered in that area. It was many years later that a deep water pipeline survey in 1986 uncovered the remains of the *Robert E. Lee* and another American freighter, the *Alcoa Puritan*. In 2001 another survey concluded that the *Alcoa Puritan* was not correctly identified but, rather, was actually the remains of the German U-boat, U-166, thought to be the only enemy submarine lost in the Gulf of Mexico during World War II. It was finally concluded that the U-166 had been initially destroyed by the depth charges near the site where it had sunk the *Robert E. Lee*. The first oil sick had meant total destruction of the submarine and the one attacked by the airmen two days later was obviously not the U-166.

Captain Wurdemann of the U-506 would later write about his experiences in the Gulf waters. He stated that success was due to surprise attacks and the fact that allied ships were unprepared to offer resistance. His submarine alone sank 10 vessels, which totaled over 60,000 tons. Fifty-six thousand of those tons were sent to the floor in the Gulf and he attributed the easy manner in which they were successful was due to the fact that no systematic observations of the sea existed; there was a lack of needed zigzagging and, the vessels lacked protection by the use of convoys.[6]

## Jim Wiggins

Also, it must be noted that many of the merchant vessels were sunk in waters off the mouth of the Mississippi River. It was a favorable atmosphere for the German enemy because of the turbid water that provided protection. It was not only muddy but the current also helped to prevent detection by sound. Though difficult to navigate in the currents, nevertheless the waters offered perfect spots for hiding.

Again, 58 ships were sunk in the Gulf between May and November of 1942. Florida was on extreme alert and had its share of the dead being washed ashore, with daily discoveries being common in some areas suitable for such by the currents and tides. Many survivors found their way to shore along Florida's beaches and many were rescued by fishermen, Coast Guard and air patrols. May, June and July were the worse months but by August, the US military had at last established a system of using heavy convoys that deterred further attack, a plan that had been long recommended by Britain. By September there was only one German U-boat, the U-171, still operating in the Gulf. It was also the submarine that was credited with having spent the longest amount of time in the Gulf. Its last target was a medium-sized tanker, the *Amatlan*. Attacks were very sporadic in 1943 and, for the most part, merchant vessels no longer felt threatened by German U-boats.

The war in the Gulf of Mexico, like that earlier in the shipping lanes of the Atlantic, was extremely rewarding for the Germans in terms of reducing the flow of supplies necessary for the war effort. Losses for the submarines were minimal. Despite the fact that access to the Gulf was confined to narrow straits and that its waters were relatively shallow, the German U-boats entered and exited the Straits of Florida and the Yucatan Channel almost at will and with few risks.

The German success in the Gulf was effective but short-lived. Britain had long been advising the US that it should incorporate the use of convoy escorts as a deterrent but production had not reached the capacity needed until late 1942. Indeed, several factors were involved in the reduction of U-boat success by the beginning of 1943. These included:

The perfection of the Huff-Duff (High Frequency Directions Finding), which enabled Allied ships to locate German submarines by their radio traffic.

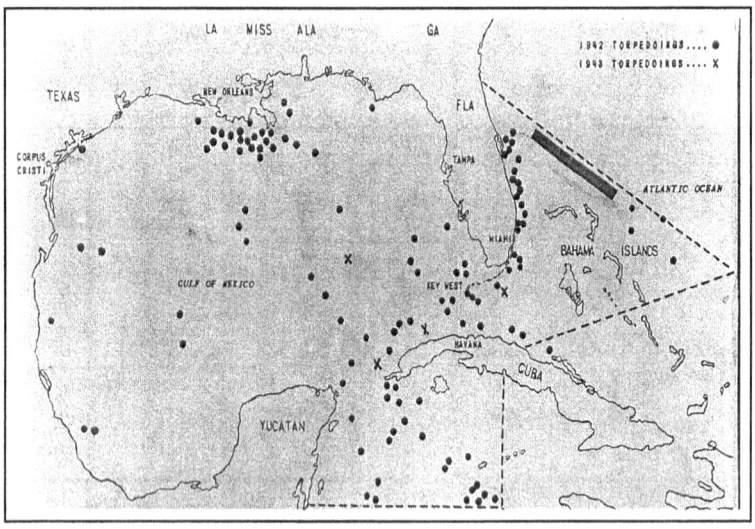

Photo 20 - This map shows the location of ships sunk in 1942 by German submarines. (*Historical Museum of Southern Florida*).

Improved radar and sonar.

More numerous escorts. This was particularly true in the Gulf where escorts made an enormous difference.

The Allies' increasing ability to read the German naval code, the "Ultra Secret."[7]

Success by the German submarines along the US Eastern

## Jim Wiggins

Seaboard and in the Gulf of Mexico was absolutely phenomenal. Floridians, in particular, had front-row seats to witness some of the most outstanding events of World War II unfolding before them. Many old-timers, like myself, lived in Florida during those turbulent years but can recall only a few bits and pieces. However, there were many first-hand participants, including those who personally witnessed warfare and explosions close offshore. Thankfully, some of their experiences were recorded. Unfortunately, most belonged to a generation that will soon be gone and their memories are now buried in the annals of passing time.

# Chapter Six

# Germans on Florida Soil

In 1942 Florida hosted what was described by one historian as "the most exciting operation in the state since the Civil War."[1] It was incomprehensible to even imagine the presence of terrorists on American soil at that time. The 9/11 attack on New York City brought the reality of terrorism home to Americans but many people do not realize that acts of terror on American soil were barely averted way back in 1942. Florida was the site where part of that plot took place. It was an undercover operation that was carefully orchestrated by the Germans and, except for unusual circumstances that thwarted the completion of the operation, could have been carried out with major consequences that would have altered the complexities of World War II. No one will ever know what the consequences of a successful mission might have been, but the failed attempt certainly is worthy of stirring up one's imagination.

Florida was in a dither after the declaration of war, not

only with the rush to complete the establishment of military bases but in its adjustments to changes that loomed everywhere. German U-boats were sinking allied ships in close offshore waters with impunity and fears were growing about America's preparedness for war. Florida was caught up in the hustle and bustle of war readiness and it was certainly not prepared to receive news of an invasion on its own beaches by Nazi saboteurs. The notion of having saboteurs on American soil was incomprehensible. That was the last news that residents wanted to hear despite all kinds of unfounded rumors about possible landings.

But on June 17, 1942, that is exactly what happened. Four Germans were delivered at night by submarine to Florida's coast and swam quietly in the warm waters to shore at Ponte Vedra Beach just south of Jacksonville. Four days earlier their counterparts had arrived on Long Island in New York. Both groups had left on separate submarines about three weeks earlier from the German base at Lorient, France. It was a carefully planned operation that was brazen but, if successful, would have doubtlessly shaken the foundation of America's sense of home security.

The Florida group included the leader, Edward John Kerling, age 33; Werner Thiel, 35; Herman Otto Neubauer, 32; and Herbert Hans Haupt, 22. They landed in their German uniforms to ensure that they would be treated as prisoners of war if caught. Otherwise, if apprehended, they could be tried as spies and sentenced to death. Their landing was not detected so they proceeded to bury their German uniforms in the sand, hoping to retrieve them later. Everything went smoothly. Who would have imagined that here they were: four German saboteurs standing on a beach in Florida! They then put on civilian clothing and made their way to Jacksonville to catch a train for Cincinnati. They would then split up in Ohio with one couple traveling on to New York and the other to Chicago. Their trip was a bold maneuver to

## Jim Wiggins

infiltrate and sabotage American war efforts.

Germany had been surprised at the ability and speed of the US to manufacture and produce goods needed for war. Their objective was the destruction of sites used for such purposes but they also felt strongly that such terrorist attacks on American soil would initiate a psychological response that would destroy the will of the citizens to wage a war. All eight of the saboteurs had been trained at a special school in Berlin for such purposes and each man had lived for some time in the United States so that they felt capable of working without threat of detection. All eight spoke perfect English and all were familiar with American customs, which would help to avoid suspicions about their illegal activity.

The four men who landed near Amagansett, Long Island, New York, did not fare as well as their counterparts in Florida. Shortly after midnight on June 13, four days earlier than the arrival in Florida, the four men landed at the direct spot that was being patrolled by John Cullen, a 21-year-old Coast Guardsman. It was a mere coincidence that their landing was at this precise location on the beach where he was standing guard. Perhaps part of the reason was due to the fact that it was a dense foggy night. Cullen observed the men and thought possibly that their bags contained clams. He approached them and requested that the men follow him to his headquarters up the beach but they refused, offering friendly gestures to the shaken young man. Finally, Dasch offered Cullen a bribe of $260 with cash that he pulled out of his pocket. Cullen took the money, backed away in the deep fog and ran to his headquarters with the report to his superiors that was hard for them to believe.

An armed patrol returned to the spot but no one was there. The four men had already left for the Amagansett train station where they caught the 6:57 to New York City. The patrol searched and found a canvas bag with German uniforms and tin boxes that held explosives, detonators and disguised bombs.

## Jim Wiggins

Everyone was shocked. America had been invaded by German spies! But no one knew at that time that four men had also landed in Florida at Ponte Vedra Beach. It was only a matter of time, however, before the whole story would be known. However, something very unusual was about to change the Germans' plans. A new twist on the story was about to emerge.

For some unknown reason, possibly because of being detected on the beach, one of the men, George Dasch, decided to inform the FBI of their plans and even went so far as to share his feelings to Ernest Burger, his friend, while they were in a Manhattan hotel. Dasch did just as he said he would and called the FBI headquarters in New York on the evening of June 14, stating that he would like to talk personally with J. Edgar Hoover. He was interrogated by agents and shared all of the information about the plot to terrorize American citizens.

Everyone was particularly surprised when he revealed the landing of four men on a beach in Florida. He shared all the information about the planned rendezvous. Two of the Florida group was arrested in New York on June 23 and the other two were arrested in Chicago four days later. It was an absolute miracle that all eight had been incarcerated without any destruction of US property. No one could fully comprehend why Dasch had made the decision to reveal the plot. Contrary to what was believed, Dasch insisted that some of the men never fully intended to follow through with the sabotage plans. The fact is that the plot probably represented a much larger conspiracy of the German-American Bund, an organization, which was intended to promote terrorism in the US by support from many Hitler loyalists. In addition to the large amount of material brought ashore by the saboteurs, a large sum of money was also found in their possession at the time of their arrest. A total of $174,588 in US currency was seized by the FBI and an additional amount of $612 had been spent for food, clothing and housing during their two weeks on American soil. There was also the additional $260 bribe that was given to young Cullen on Ponte Vedra Beach. It is likely that most of the expenditures would have been used for equipment and materials to be designed for destruction of America's war machines such as factories and infrastructure necessary for war efforts. The exact extent of the intentions, however, would never be fully known if the original plot had been carried out. A Military Commission composed of seven US Army officers appointed by President Roosevelt held trial and all eight were condemned to death. However, Attorney General Frances Biddle and J. Edgar Hoover interceded on behalf of Dasch and Burger because of their cooperation and, as a result, their sentence was reduced to 30 years each.

In April of 1948 President Truman granted clemency to both men, who were deported to Germany. In 1952 Dasch told a reporter that he was perceived as a traitor in his homeland and was treated badly. He also stated that he had personally spared the life of Cullen, the young patrol, on that evening in New York despite orders that required anyone should be killed who threatened the success of their mission. Cullen later stated that Dasch wasn't really a bad guy or else his life wouldn't have been spared. Floridians might well wonder why espionage was not planned for military operations in Florida instead of northern cities. No other location in the United States held more sites designed for war efforts than did Florida. In fact, the team that landed on Florida's shoreline was within striking distance of numerous spots such as those at nearby Jacksonville and both coasts were dotted with new installations of airfields and training bases, including shipyards. Of course, the plot was foiled long before it actually got off the ground and no one really knows what might have been in the making of this misguided act of espionage. Perhaps the targeting of big cities with large populations was just one way to affect more Americans and to gain the attention of the country's citizens.

## Jim Wiggins

For the most part, Florida cities were still sparsely populated and all of the military targets were never concentrated in one locality but, rather, were sprinkled throughout the state. Thankfully, the scheme failed and no one will ever know what might have been.

The invasion into Florida territory is just one of the many unusual happenings during those crucial and frightening years when no one knew for certain where the enemy might strike. Indeed, all of us were urged to report any unusual or suspicious activity and every Floridian was constantly reminded of possible threats to our security. But for most of us kids it was all just a natural part of daily life. We were all immersed in wartime living but could not fully comprehend the true realities in a war being fought somewhere else. In fact, I cannot recall that any information was ever released about the landing of real-life saboteurs on Florida soil until well after the fact. Perhaps such an announcement would have been too much to handle by Floridians who were already witnessing ships being blown up along their shorelines.

However, the four men who landed on Ponte Vedra Beach were not the only German soldiers who visited Florida during the war. Approximately 10,000 German prisoners of war were located in Florida. These POWS were among the 378,000 incarcerated throughout the US. Information about these camps located in 45 states for enemy detainees was not made available to the general public. Robert D. Billinger, Jr., author of the informative book, *Hitler's Soldiers in the Sunshine State: German POWs in Florida*, offers reasons for the lack of information released by the US Government:

> *There were, of course, the provisions of the 1939 Geneva Convention regarding the handling of prisoners of war that were to protect prisoners, 'against acts of violence, insults and public curiosity.' But there was also the real concern that*

> *public awareness would bring either public fear or public criticism of government handling of the POWs and inhibit the most efficient use of POW labor within the United States. Thus, the officially sanctioned and later tolerated press coverage of the POW program was relatively sparse. It took three forms: government-sponsored, and thus very positive, often pictorial, articles in national journals and newspapers, local newspaper coverage regarding the labor contributions, potential or real to local economies, and the relatively infrequent and brief physical descriptions and mug shots of escaped POWs, whose public identification and recapture was the official task of the FBI. The result was that few citizens in wartime America, with the exception of military guards and civilian employers of the POWs were aware of their presence.[2]*

Billinger rightly points out that the earliest historical studies of POWs on American soil didn't begin until the 1970s and even by the 1980s was restricted to coverage of larger camps such as those in Alabama, Louisiana, Virginia, North Carolina, and Indiana. His provocative portrayal of Florida POWs describes the uniqueness of its 26 camps with particular emphasis on Camp Blanding in North Florida near Starke. One unique feature was the diversity of the prisoners who held distinctive political and moral views. Distinctions between "Nazi" and "anti-Nazi" bewildered prisoners and captors alike and led to conflicts affecting the welfare of everyone. Too, the POW camps in Florida were unique by what Bellinger calls the "regional component." He writes:

> *Because of its climate and geography, conducive agriculture, forestry, and military bases...as well as to tourism...Florida had an uncommon variety of locales, economics and animal life for POWs to confront. Due to this variety, the Florida experience*

*was the American POW experience in sunnier microcosm with additional unique factors thrown in. German POWs in Florida represented the wide variety of military formations, units, political factions and nationalities found in Hitler's forces. They worked on military bases, in timbering and in agriculture, just as POWs did throughout America. But they also picked citrus crops, harvested*

Photo 21 - German POWS learn English in a classroom at Camp Blanding. (*Florida Archives*)

*sugarcane in snake-infested fields, and worked in Miami Beach resort hotels like no other POWs did in America.*[3]

The first German prisoners assigned to Florida arrived in September, 1942. Only a few naval men who had been rescued from sunken submarines were incarcerated at Camp Blanding but their uniqueness required utmost secrecy by intelligence officers who sought to interrogate them at a time when German submarines were actively destroying allied ships almost without resistance. These first POWs consisted of only two officers and 12 seamen who came from four German submarines destroyed in 1942: J-701, U-210, U-94, and U-162. However, Britain would soon be overwhelmed with the task of housing prisoners in its bombed-out landscape and soon the US would be saturated with POW camps. Residents would include naval men who were a special breed in themselves.

Many of the German soldiers were intrigued with Florida's tropical setting, illustrated by their fascination in capturing snakes for the taking of skins as souvenirs. Most enjoyed the sunshine and warm climate and became adept at catching fish in the numerous rivers and lakes that abounded in the Sunshine State. Flower and vegetable gardens were planted and the surroundings of the camps were kept tidy because of the fastidious habits of many prisoners. Supervisors and employers of work crews seldom complained and were amazed at the manner in which the POWs accepted responsibility for their chores.

Of course, each situation was different, depending upon the location of the camp and the type of work assigned. For example, work at Clewiston in the harvesting of sugar cane with machetes in burned fields was particularly hard. No comparison could be made with those working shifts at a hotel setting in Miami Beach with amenities such as swimming in the ocean and sleeping in comfortable beds. In each case the allotted pay was eighty cents per eight-hour day. The assignments were simply based on the luck of the cards, which might be harvesting cane, picking citrus, repairing equipment, construction, pulpwork, gathering vegetables, washing dishes, or any other of the menial tasks needed by a shortage of American laborers.

The US Government sought to enforce rules of the Geneva Convention by meeting its standards, but was criticized by some for making life too easy for enemy POWs while American soldiers were being mistreated in German camps. A contingent at

Belle Glade, for example, went on strike because of a delay in cigarette allotments and this act resulted in accusations that German POWs were being spoiled rotten. A Tampa newspaper even went so far as to list camp menus at MacDill and contended that prisoners were being given better treatment than American GIs. African American GIs complained that the German prisoners were given better treatment than they were in their segregated barracks, a complaint that, unfortunately, was very true.

Despite a general feeling of contentment by most Florida

Photo 22 - German POWS pick oranges in central Florida. (*US National Archives*)

POWs, there were attempted escapes.[4] But these were quite limited in number. One young man, Karl Behrens, escaped from the Clewiston camp and was found hanging from a nearby tree on December 30, 1944. Eleven escapes took place at Camp

## Jim Wiggins

Blanding, five from Dade City, four at Clewiston, two at Kendall, two by the same individual at Orlando, one at Winter Haven, one at Daytona, one at MacDill, two from Camp Gordon Johnston, and four at one time from Telogia. Several of the soldiers had become seasoned escapees.[5]

One of the most touching stories about escaped German POWs comes from Tampa when it was announced that Johann Klapper, age 49, had escaped from the MacDill camp. His escape came in March, 1946, after the end of the war when German POWs were being repatriated back to Europe. The *Tampa Morning Tribune* gave a detailed description of the man and stated that he had been a farmer with a wife and five children. Surprisingly, the man was discovered three months later in a burrow beneath one of the MacDill buildings. He had existed by drinking from a trickle of water leaking through the floor below an icebox and food was salvaged by scrounging in garbage bins. The dirty and bearded soldier was not aware that his comrades had already been returned to Europe.

By and large, the German POW camps in Florida proved to be successful. Indeed, their work was thorough; problems were somewhat minimal and their contributions to the economy were noteworthy. Unlike the four spies who landed at Ponte Vedra voluntarily for acts of terror, the POWs came to Florida involuntarily but ended up by making favorable contributions. Indeed, the whole process appeared almost congenial. There were exceptions, of course, but the positive elements appear to far outweigh the negative, summed up ably by Robert Billinger:

> *Healthy young men with smiling faces were working in the Florida sunshine. The faces were German. During the day their owners wore US Army fatigues with distinctive white PW lettering, but at night they returned to variants of their weathered Wehmacht uniforms. They were Americans...or almost...by*

> day, Hitler's soldiers by night. They led two lives.
> But it is the smiling faces that are most remembered
> by the 'alumni' of the POW program in Florida. In
> light of the fact that Hitler's soldiers in Florida
> revealed the ideological, social, and psychological
> cleavages that ran deep below the veneer of Nazi
> ideological uniformity and German military
> discipline, it seems odd to focus first on a work
> program that provided Germans and Americans
> with happy memories and the idea that enemies are
> human. However, pleasant memories that effaced
> earlier adversarial stereotypes were part of an
> evolving cognitive process. It was a stage in the
> changing mutual perceptions that remained an
> important impact of the wartime experiences on the
> lives of participants. Preconceptions that all of
> Hitler's soldiers were Nazis were replaced in the
> minds of many Floridians with an equally
> generalized image of the smiling boy next door. A
> similar process took place among the POWs.
> Americans, particularly guards and American
> civilians with whom they had contact during work
> experiences, began to be seen as fellow workers,
> comrades, or even friends.[6]

Billinger goes on to emphasize that some stereotypes did remain in spite of positive changes.[7] That, of course, would be expected, particularly among those diehards who were totally devoted to Hitler's Nazi Germany. But, for the most part, postwar writings and visits made on return trips, indicate that goodwill by POWs located in Florida far exceeded what could have been expected from enemy prisoners.

Only two of the German men who landed on American soil as saboteurs were allowed to live and ultimately return to their homeland. In contrast, most of the POWs returned to their homeland with stories of a beautiful and tropical land where friends were plentiful, food and housing were adequate and where fair play was practiced by their captors. These stories were a far cry from that which was heard by returning American GIs who witnessed atrocities in German war camps. Floridians, in particular, can be extremely proud of the role they played in this unique wartime exchange.

# Chapter Seven

# Florida's Economic Expansion

Though Florida witnessed unusual real estate deals being completed before 1941 for the procurement and expansion of military bases, no one fully appreciated the fact that the Sunshine State was standing on the threshold of such tremendous economic change. Floridians had chosen Spessard L. Holland of Bartow as their governor in 1940 but he had inherited a large bonded debt bequeathed to him by the booming 1920s, including $1 1/2 million dollars of unpaid bills for expanded state administration and services. That amount of state indebtedness was considered a large sum by standards of that day. Governor Holland proposed a two cents per gallon tax on gasoline for the next fifty years for the payment of debts and construction of roads. He also introduced legislation for tax reform. Wartime restrictions on gasoline and pari-mutuel betting reduced tax income but building restrictions allowed greater revenue to be saved for other projects such as teacher salaries and social needs. The wartime revenue increased to such a degree in Florida that Governor Holland was eventually able to leave a balance of some $8 million in the general fund and an additional $14 million for road building at the end of his term.

Defense installations called for additional spending and the federal government paid for the costs of priority materials. During Governor Holland's four-year governorship the Florida

## Jim Wiggins

State Road Department built 1,560 miles of highway at a cost of over $44 million, of which $15,394,851 was paid by the federal government. By 1945 there were over 8,000 miles of highway. Most of these roads were necessary to provide military access and Floridians were fortunate in having them subsidized with federal expenditures.

Almost every aspect of production became essential during the war years. Florida was particularly favored because agricultural needs were at an all-time high. Vegetables being shipped out to provide food for troops was just as important as the laying of steel girders in a shipyard designed to build weapons of war. Historian John Keegan aptly expressed this sentiment by stating, "Supply of food, of raw materials, of finished products, of weapons themselves, lies at the root of war."[1] Florida was at the "root of war" in many ways, supplying in great quantities the fruits and vegetables so direly needed, as well as actively participating in the procurement of raw materials and the manufacture of finished products so necessary in the war effort. Florida soon exceeded all other states in providing fresh fruits and vegetables for the military during all the war years.

"Rosie the Riveter" became a dominant symbol during those years as women were relegated to jobs previously served by men. Workers were in demand everywhere at all levels of employment but nowhere was the shortage more critical than at shipyards. The production of ships was an extremely high priority and no other state in the US was given such responsibility as was given to Florida. Florida shipyards included the Tampa Shipbuilding and Engineering Company (later known as TASCO), the Hooker's Point Shipyard in Tampa, the Wainwright Shipyard in Panama City, the St. Johns River Shipyard Company, the Miami Shipbuilding Corporation, the Pensacola Shipyard and Engineering Company, a shipbuilding company in Orlando, and other small operations. "Alligator" amphibious vehicles were produced at Dunedin and activity pervaded the state.

As early as the mid-1930s the US Government recognized the importance of shipbuilding and as hostilities increased in Europe was made more aware of the need to expand facilities in

Photo 23 - The Tampa Shipyards grew quickly until they were employing 20,000 workers. (*Florida Archives*)

Florida, which had served a need during World War I and beyond. As early as 1936 the Merchant Marine Act provided financial assistance to the Tampa Shipbuilding and engineering Company (TASCO) with the award of $8 million for the building of four new cargo ships. This act alone resulted in jobs for 2,000 persons and as the threat of war increased, so did the orders for additional building.

A dry dock was completed in Tampa and old ships were soon to be renovated for new use. Naval vessels such as ammunition cargo ships, destroyer tenders, coastal mine sweepers, destroyer escorts, cargo ships, repair ships and coastal patrol boats were soon coming off the assembly line and with the bombing of

## Jim Wiggins

Pearl Harbor the production increased sizably. Old men, teenagers, and an increasing number of women joined forces to meet the demands for vessels of warfare, raising the number employed at Tampa to more than 20,000 workers.

The housing problem was severe in Tampa and elsewhere, not only because of the vast numbers of employees at the shipyards, but also for the increasing units of military men with their families at emerging airbases.

> With the influx of thousands of workers, Tampa and other Florida cities' civic leaders were pressed to locate suitable housing. Added to the situation in many cases was the demand for more housing by nearby military installations.
>
> Many ideas were suggested including turning vacant factory buildings into suitable apartments and establishing trailer parks. Eventually the shipbuilding companies and the cities supplied municipal housing, which helped alleviate some of the problem, but it was always crowded. In addition to the TASCO yards, Tampa Marine, located along the Ybor Channel, produced 98 sea-going fleet tugs for the Navy. Bushnell-Lyons produced large, steel cargo barges for the Navy. The Navy, realizing the need to house personnel or troops in various war zones, converted many of the barges or lighters, into floating barracks ships.[2]

Tampa had been instrumental in building concrete ships during World War I at the Hooker's Point Yard. Matthew H. McCloskey, owner of a large Philadelphia construction company, argued that concrete ships might well be used again by the US as a substitute for the shortage of steel, pointing out that they might serve well against the attacks by the German U-boats which had been causing so much damage in shipping lanes. The Florida Portland Cement Company was not far from the port and

## Jim Wiggins

McCloskey insisted that the ships could be built more efficiently with the use of a product called Fullers Earth, a light-weight clay that could be mixed with the sand.

The resulting concrete ships were powered by 3,500-horsepower engines and did quite well. Several were sent to Normandy where two were sunk and used as beachheads. My hometown of Ellenton had once been the site of the Fullers Earth Plant, which became one of south Florida's largest industries in the early 1900s. When McCloskey initiated the production of cement ships, a crew returned to Ellenton to determine whether or not it would be feasible to restart the old plant along the Manatee River at Rocky Bluff. A team of experts arrived with heavy equipment and began digging in search of new veins of the clay-like substance commonly used as an absorbent for grease in filters. (Interestingly enough, the small team turned to my father when they ran into the problem of water seeping into the areas being excavated. My father was hired for several weeks to bring his sump pump to the site to drain the water.) However, the attempt to rekindle mining at the Ellenton site proved futile and was quickly abandoned.

The demand for concrete ships ebbed soon after Henry J. Kaiser began building the popular Liberty Ship, which could be off the assembly line in less than two weeks.

The Gibbs Shipyards, located on the south side of the St. Johns River in Jacksonville had supplied naval ships during World War I. Its expansion ceased at the end of the war and for many years sat dormant and in decay. However, the pre-war years of World War II ushered in a new demand and the yards were renovated to provide for future needs.

*The Gibbs yard was involved in the production of over a hundred different types of vessels from the PT boats to landing craft of every size and shape. The speedy wooden-hulled PT boats became the*

## Jim Wiggins

*yard's specialty. Many of the boats were sent to the British as part of the Lend Lease program to aid in the on-going Channel war. These boats were used in all theaters of war for a variety of purposes. A PT training base was maintained at Mayport throughout the war. The use of millions of sea mines by both sides in the war required the use of many wooden-hulled mine sweepers...the so-called YMS, the Yard Mine Sweeper.*[3]

Tampa and Jacksonville were not the only two sites used for shipbuilding. The Prigg Boat Works in Miami produced small boats and ships, notably the 110-foot PC submarine chaser.

Another very important shipbuilding site was dedicated on May 22, 1942, which included participants Governor Spessard Holland and US Senators Claude Pepper, Charles O. Anderson and Congressman Bob Sikes. It was the Panama City Wainwright Shipyard where the famed EC-2 Liberty Ship and the "T" tankers were made. The Liberty Ship was a 444-foot cargo transport with three decks, weighing 11,000 pounds and able to travel at a speed of 10 knots when fully loaded. Thirty-three were built at Panama City and proved to be sturdy workhorses for the Navy. Six "T" tankers, 500 feet in length, were also built at the Panama City Shipyards.

The site selected in Panama City was Dyers Point, about one mile south of the eastern end of Hathaway Bridge. The location offered deep water and 4,700 feet of bayfront shoreline, a deal completed when a contract was made with J.A. Jones Company of Charlotte, North Carolina, for the operation of a 72-acre site at a cost of $62 million. The government leased the land from the railroad for 10 years with the understanding that the Jones company would build a spur railroad to the site. The contract called for the construction of six areas for launching ships and about 70 buildings that included headquarters, offices, police and fire departments and numerous classrooms for training. The shipyard was originally called the Panama City Shipbuilding Corporation but was renamed for Gen. Jonathan Wainwright, a defender of Bataan and prisoner of war.

During the early years of World War II shipbuilding became the largest industry in Florida. The influx of workers was astronomical. Most of the workers were necessarily confined to the immediate areas surrounding their work because of the great shortages of tires and gasoline for travel. Many used the railroads for travel back to their homes during rare breaks from work and this meant sharing in crowded aisles with military men and women traveling back and forth from their bases to home. Tent cities were erected everywhere to provide housing for workers' families and campgrounds seemed to spring up across the state almost every day to meet the increasing demand for Florida's bulging population.

The Pensacola Navy Yard had a long history that dates back to 1826 when it was constructed, becoming one of the best-equipped naval stations in the United States. It was used at that time primarily as a deterrent to the slave trade and piracy in the Gulf and Caribbean. In 1862 most of the yard was destroyed by Confederates when New Orleans was captured by Union forces, fearing that they would take it over. An aviation training station was established there in 1912 and was the only naval station during World War I. At the end of the war in 1918, 436 officers and 5,538 enlisted men were stationed there and over 1,000 naval aviators graduated from the school. The US Naval Air Station was expanded by 1940 and more than 1,000 cadets were being trained each month during the war years.

Florida's giant oak trees had been used in the building of ships during earlier years and the US Federal Government had even planted trees in northern parts of the state so that the large curved "bents" could be used for the U-hulled shapes. Modern times soon required the use of steel, which superseded previous needs for wood. However, in the early 1940s there was a demand for the use of Florida's cypress trees in the building of small boats. Cuttings took place without regard for environmental or conservation concerns as large landowners pounced upon meeting the demands of the government.

Cypress, mahogany, and other trees also became objects of lust in the early 1940's. During World War II, cypress was used to make PT boats, and loggers began to move into the Big Cypress Swamp to destroy its centuries-old trees. A few years later, after World War II, manufacturers demanded cypress for coffins, barrels, decks for houses, stadium bleachers, boats, and paneling; and the timber company...the Lee Tidewater, and J.C. Turner companies chief among them...pushed deeper into the wilderness.[4]

The expanded need for oil during the war pushed companies to explore for resources in Florida. Exploration had already begun at the turn of the century in the Pensacola area with drillings that reached 10,000 feet without success. In fact, an offer of $50,000 was the prize for any company that was able to produce oil in Florida. On September 26, 1943, Florida's first successful oil well flowed at Sunniland Field in northern Collier County. The Humble Oil Company found oil at 11,626 feet and by 1945 would be producing about a half million barrels annually.

A process for the use of frozen concentrate citrus was developed by Dr. L.G. McDowell of the Florida Citrus Commission and Dr. Arthur L. Stahl of the University of Florida Agricultural Experimental Station and this was a great gain to the industry. Interesting enough, a product, DDT, that was discovered by the Germans in 1874, was introduced to Florida in 1942 and began to be used extensively in Florida agriculture. It was introduced into the armed forces to combat mosquitoes, lice and other disease carrying insects. Its residual quality was praised highly and it was not until years later that the negative impact of this dangerous chemical was realized.

The Florida Defense Council was created in World War I by Governor Catts but was re-created during World War II to include 4-F and older citizens to serve in capacities such as air raid wardens and medical assistants. They also served in numerous acts of enforcement such as monitoring blackouts, rationing, or volunteering as air and U-boat spotters. They served on the local front in fire and police auxiliary units and contributed in many ways to the war effort. Indeed, every available able-bodied youth,

Photo 24 - Wooden ships are being built at the Oscar Daniels Shipyard in Tampa. (*Florida Archives*)

man or woman was put to good use. The Civil Air Patrol, organized in March of 1942, helped to patrol Florida's coasts and the "Mosquito Fleet" operated out of bases such as Jacksonville, Fort Lauderdale, Key West, St. Petersburg and Pensacola. The so-called "Donald Duck Navy" trained more than 10,000 US officers and 37,000 enlisted men at the Miami submarine-Chaser Training School at Miami. 360 officers and over 10,000 men from 14 other countries were also trained in Miami at this school during the years of 1942 and 1943.

Not only were there a quarter of a million men and women in uniform from Florida during the Second World War, there were many other heroes involved in the war effort. For example, the longest air route during the war originated in Florida. Planes flew from the Sunshine State to Brazil, across the South Atlantic to the Gold Coast, crossed Africa to India, and through the Netherlands East Indies to the Philippines or Australia, or through Burma and its mountains into China. All planes for the Near East, India and China began in Florida, many originating at Morrison Field in West Palm Beach or on civilian contract flights from Miami. Pan American Airlines had an Africa-Orient Division, commonly referred to as the "Cannon Ball Express," which opened in 1942 and flew from Miami to Karachi, India, with cargo for Burma and China. This division alone made 2,300 crossings of the Atlantic on military missions and logged more than 14.5 million miles in less than a year. Each trip took only three-and-one-half days.[5]

Eastern Airlines also began to make daily contract flights from Miami to Trinidad in May of 1942 and later extended their operations to include Natal, Brazil and Accra on the Gold Coast of Africa. They flew for the US Air Transport Command and eventually covered nearly 34 million miles and carried nearly 47 million pounds of cargo, including 130,000 passengers.[6] National Airlines, Delta, and United Airlines also participated in contract flights during the war years. In each case, these airlines were subsidized heavily by the contracts with the federal government and it is unlikely that any could have survived without this added revenue at a time when civilian travel was restricted.

# Chapter Eight

# The Home Front

As already stated, Florida stood upon the precipice of extreme change unlike any other state in the US. One historian summed it up well:

> During the Second World War, playground Florida became Campground USA as airmen and sailors came to train quickly in the warmth and ship out. Resort hotels on both coasts were converted to barracks; calisthenics were conducted on the beaches where the beauties bathed; jungle survival and landing courses met in the Everglades and along the Keys, where poisonous plants and snakes were among the hazards. At Miami Beach seventy thousand hotel rooms were requisitioned by the Army Air Force; Flagler's Ponce de Leon Hotel in St. Augustine served the Coast Guard. There were new military bases at Tampa and Orlando, revived ports at Key West and Pensacola, an airfield at

*Homestead. Dirigibles patrolled the coast, looking for U-boats, while destroyers stood offshore to intercept them. Airmen on training flights over the Everglades dumped their cigarette butts out the bomb bays and ignited the dried-out sawgrass and muck. Farm workers deserted the fields for factory jobs or served in the military in such great numbers that migrants were brought from the Bahamas and other islands to cut sugarcane and pick fruit and vegetables. Students too young to fight were sent along with prisoners to help in the harvest. Women worked the factories and mills. Shipbuilding contracts brought new wealth to the dry docks at Tampa and Jacksonville.*[1]

Historian Gary Mormino described the war as a "cornucopia" for Floridians who were waiting to reap all kinds of goodies, pointing out that "The war poured huge sums of money into Florida's underdeveloped narrowly based economy."[2]

Perhaps one of the greatest reality checks came on September 16, 1940, when President Roosevelt signed into law the Selective Training and Service Act, which set up the first peacetime military draft in US history. This happened after the fall of France and the German siege on British landmarks, placing a sense of urgency on the president to insure US readiness for whatever was coming.

At this point it should be noted that Florida's Senator Claude Pepper played a highly important role in supporting legislation for intervention in the war. He was one of the major spokesmen for allied support as a member of the Committee on Foreign Relations. He and his wife traveled to Germany in 1938 and reported back to President Roosevelt that Adolph Hitler's military regime was definitely a threat to the security of the world. He drafted the Lend Lease resolution designed to provide military equipment to allied forces, a plan that was twice rejected by the

## Jim Wiggins

US Senate but was finally passed in 1941. He also supported the 1940 plan for Selective Service and received the outrage of citizens, primarily mothers, who hanged him in effigy in front of the US Capitol.[3]

Initially, men between 21 to 35 years of age were required to register in the first stages of the draft. This age grouping was limited in scope but offered an immediate boost in the military that was not yet prepared to accept larger numbers. This initiated the procedure for drafting more than 10 million men into the military during the years of World War II. Of course, this act of Congress was amended several times as the demand for recruits increased.

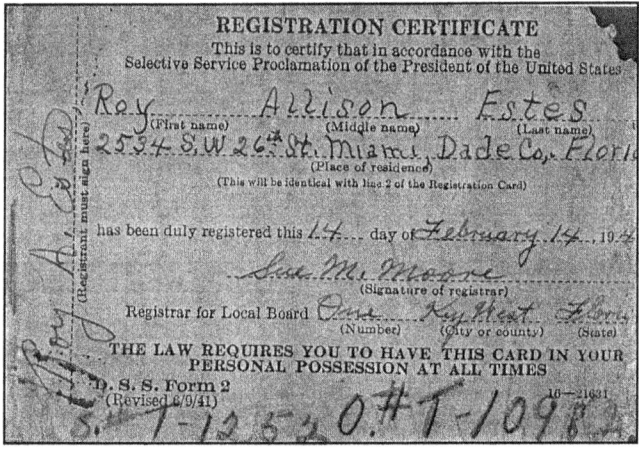

Photo 25 - Shown here is the draft card of Roy Estes of Miami, which is typical of those issued by local selective service boards. (*Florida Archives*)

Volunteers initially stepped forward in great numbers after the bombing of Pearl Harbor but as time passed so did the need for an increasing number of men.

The Florida National Guard had already been instituted in 1939 with 3,000 recruits from Florida and was called into active national military service between November 1940 and January 1941. Florida's National Guard units were initially a part of the

## Jim Wiggins

31st Infantry Division and was nicknamed the "Dixie Division" because its composition included guard units from several southern states.

Camp Blanding served as the training site from late 1940 through mid-1941. Most local communities knew someone in the National Guard. For example, all of us were aware in our community that our local principal's son, Buddy Meade, was an active officer in the local unit. I can still recall seeing the principal shed tears in the classroom on the day that he left for his training. Many Florida guardsmen were reassigned to different units and fought in every campaign of the war in Europe and the Pacific. Those remaining in the 31st Division earned distinguished unit citations for their excellent performance. At least 158 guardsmen from Florida died during the war. A Florida State Guard, composed primarily of old and 4F citizens, was established to assume the duties of the departed guardsmen and by 1943 this group numbered 2,100 men in 36 units.

Anxiety over the draft plagued most families, particularly since each county in Florida, like elsewhere in the US, had certain quotas to meet, resulting in a lot of inequities. For example, in 1940 married men were being drafted in one county while only single men were being drafted in others. Some who escaped the draft in 1940 were suddenly listed as 1A in 1941 and 1942 so there was no degree of certainty that one's status would be retained over a period of time. In 1940 it was rather easy to be deferred but after the start of the war this became increasingly difficult and by 1942 the demand was so great that only the most disabled were listed as 4F or were being deferred for some reason such as being in a vocation necessary to serve the war effort. Included in that group were farmers while jobs at shipyards and military bases were rapidly being filled by women. Rejection from military duty for having flat feet was jokingly used to describe deferments for health reasons. By 1943 and 1944, most men between the ages of

18 and 45 were expected to serve.

One interesting story about the draft involved the Neff family. Mr. and Mrs. William H. Neff decided to hide their son, Morris Stanley, in their home when he turned 21 and was being called up by the draft for military duty. The deception was discovered and the family went for a hearing with a grand jury where it was revealed that the young man had been hidden in his room for three years. He stated to the Assistant District Attorney

Photo 26 - Mr. And Mrs. William H. Neff and their son, Morris, appear before a grand jury on charges that Morris was hidden for 3 years in his home to avoid the draft. (*Florida Archives*)

Fred Botts that it was his parents' idea and that he would have been willing to be drafted. His safety in hiding was enhanced when his parents discontinued claiming him as a dependent by securing ration stamps in his name.

Young Neff, of course, was the rare exception. Most young men could hardly wait to sign up. Patriotism was always in the air and the draft was just part of the whole scheme of things. As an adolescent I recall hearing older high school boys speaking of signing up and going off to war as a very macho thing, somewhat akin to stories heard today about Middle East volunteers signing up for suicide missions. National pride and patriotic duty were combined to offer a major incentive for being one of the first to sign up. Of course, after much of the reality set in about harsh training in boot camp and the actual dangers of war, young men weren't quite so ready to speed things up. However, few could escape the threat of induction and there seemed to be little incentive for trying to avoid the inevitable. The term "draft-dodger" was not held in good repute but was reserved only for the rare few who used family wealth and political clout to forestall induction into military service. True conscientious objectors were the exception and were assigned to positions which didn't include combat duty.

My father, for example, was in his early 40s and had been deferred because of his status as a farmer. But the war crisis became increasingly severe and additional men were badly needed by 1943 so he was suddenly given the preferred status of a 1A card, indicating that he would be drafted. Assuming that he would not be able to harvest his crops, he chose not to plant in the fall. Conscription was delayed, however, and in order to meet family expenses, he left temporarily to work in the new oil fields of the Everglades. He narrowly escaped the draft because of his age, family obligations and his necessary role as a farmer supplying food for the war effort. But it was a close call. The same was true of many other farmers in Florida. The Sunshine State was one of the major contributors of fruits and vegetables for the war cause and the persons who were primarily responsible were small truck farmers like my father. It was with a great sigh of relief that he was able to continue in his vocation, particularly at the close of the war when the end was in sight.

The loss of more than 248,000 Florida men to the war was not the only thing noticeable on the home front. Dramatic changes

## Jim Wiggins

were everywhere. The draft was no respecter of persons. Social or economic status made no difference. Women and older residents joined auxiliary organizations and patriotism became a way of life for everyone who tried in some way to make their contribution to the cause. Volunteers joined at the headquarters of the Red Cross to package bandages and to sew while schools, churches and organizations rallied to call forth its people to serve in whatever capacity they could to help the cause of war.

Rubber became the first item to be rationed by the Federal Government's Office of Price Administration (OPA) in early 1942. Tires for autos and trucks became scarce and it was not unusual to see vehicles pulled over on the side of the road while the driver proceeded to pull out his patch kit for repairs. Those were the days of inner tubes and every home garage seemed to have one or two discarded ones hanging on the wall for use by kids for the making of slingshots. Of course, no child would have asked for a new inner tube for his bicycle since it was already predetermined that none were available. Every child like myself learned how to patch inner tubes and I recall that all of our bicycle tubes were practically held together by patches.

Inner tubes weren't the only things that were patched. Mothers made sure that our clothes held together with patches at a time when needles and threads were used almost daily in every household. Colorful flour sacks were converted into skirts, window curtains, or stitched together for sheets or bedspreads during the Great Depression and almost every family had already learned the secrets of scrimping and scraping for survival. Socks were darned and cuffs were stitched up or let down, depending upon whether the "dungarees" were being handed to someone bigger or smaller.

Depression glass had already been collected over the years from detergent or cereal boxes and these free items donned the tables in most homes. Of course, much of this frugal activity had

## Jim Wiggins

already been put into operation during the years of the depression when it became a necessity. Fortunately, it came in handy as a preparation for sacrifices also needed during the war years. This is not to indicate that Floridians felt the strain of added economic sacrifices during the war years. Indeed, the opposite was true. People, for the most part, were far better off during the war years in Florida than they had ever been before. Any degree of sacrifice simply came from trying to conserve goods of all kinds because of the added needs of the military.

Beginning on December 1, 1942, gasoline was rationed.

Photo 27 - The first stamps for gasoline rationing were issued on December 1, 1942. (*Florida Archives*)

People were issued A, B, or C stickers, which allowed them a certain number of gallons to be purchased each week. One's occupation determined the amount. Those with A stickers were allowed only four gallons of gas per week, decreased later to three gallons a week when shortages became more acute. Those with C stickers were allowed adequate purchases for use in their occupation, which was deemed necessary for the war effort. Almost everyone in my community, including my father, was

## Jim Wiggins

issued a C sticker for their use of a truck for agricultural purposes. Indeed, I can recall once when my father drove us three miles to Bradenton for an ice cream cone on a Sunday afternoon and Dad was chastised by a neighbor for using gasoline in such a hapless manner. Rules were strictly enforced and everyone felt obligated to adhere to those rules because it was their patriotic duty. Complaints would have brought one's patriotism in question and that was certainly never an issue with anyone that we knew.

Most of the gas used by our family truck (few families had

Photo 28 - Gov. Spessard L. Holland views defense posters in 1943. (*Florida Archives*)

two vehicles as is common today) went for hauling produce to the auction platform in nearby Palmetto, two miles away, or for driving to the Farmers Market in Tampa. Also, my father made regular deliveries to the Frazier wholesale coolers in St. Petersburg but little gas was used because the travel across Tampa Bay was made on one of the three ferryboats that hauled vehicles across the bay before the advent of the Skyway Bridge.

## Jim Wiggins

Food rationing, including sugar, began in April of 1942. Rules were strict right from the start. Residents were even asked how much sugar was in their house at the time of rationing and this amount was deducted from their first book of stamps. Honesty seemed to be part of one's patriotic duty and, amazingly, residents readily accepted the obligation of revealing what was in their cupboards. At least, so it seemed. This was followed by coffee, meats, butter, canned goods, dried peas and beans and other products. Those in our community were fortunate, however, to belong to farming households. Many people owned cows so milk and butter were readily available and food from farms was plentiful. For some reason I do recall that we occasionally bought oleo, which came in blocks of colorless lard and became yellow by mixing a package of some orange powdery substance. I'm not sure when or why we used this but perhaps it was a period when the old cow was dry or whatever. I do remember mixing the oleo and enjoying the magical color that appeared.

I also recall when the first ration books were issued. It was the main topic of conversation at the church after services as housewives discussed their use. Instructions and comments written on the cover of the first book issued were as follows:

> *Your first ration book has been issued to you, originally containing 28 war ration stamps. Other books may be issued at later dates. The following instructions apply to your first book and will apply to later books, unless otherwise ordered by the Office of Price Administration. In order to obtain a later book, the first book must be turned in. You should preserve War Rations Books with the greatest possible care.*[4]

Twelve sets of instructions followed, including the fact that only the person named could use the book, nor would stamps be accepted if they were mutilated with more than half missing.

## Jim Wiggins

Stamps were to be detached in the presence of the storekeeper and were otherwise void. The Ration Week began at Saturday midnight and continued to the following week. The book had to be turned in if the owner was in the hospital for more than 10 days and had to be returned when a person died.

Ration books were guarded like family treasures and the utmost caution was taken to care for them. Our family ration books were kept in the same drawer with our best silverware and were handled with special care. Lost or stolen books required a special compensation ordered by a county commission and books were not readily replaced without thorough investigation. No one I knew ever lost a book or allowed them to be mutilated. I do recall once that a glass of water was spilled over one of the ration books and my father's response was similar to that of having gravy spilled on his best suit. After all, those little coupons determined whether the family ate well or not.

Of course, no patriotic American would hoard items. But I do know of one dear aunt who was always afraid of shortages and proceeded to use up every stamp whether it was needed or not. Dad used to tease her a bit about hoarding and claimed that her closet shelves held enough food to feed an army. One pair of shoes was allowed per year and I remember that she came upon an extra coupon with which she purchased another pair and put them away, declaring "One never knows when they might be needed in an emergency." It was estimated that 90 percent of all civilian goods were rationed by the end of the war. Most everything that one ate, wore, or used was being rationed. Of course, for those of us fortunate enough to belong to farm families this was not the case.

I don't remember any sacrifices being made because of food shortages in our family, particularly because of our farm products, which were always available during the fall and winter months. During the summer we had an adequate supply of

## Jim Wiggins

mangoes and we regularly gathered scallops on the flats of Terra Ceia Bay, dug clams and managed to have fish available for at least one or two meals per week. Our own family used guavas in every manner conceivable: guava preserves, guava jelly, guava cake, guava bread, guava jam and fresh guavas that could be picked almost everywhere. Blackberries and scuppernong grapes were in abundance and clumps of sugar cane grew at the edge of our back property. Almost every household in our community had a pressure cooker for canning and most household wives had already received instructions from the county agents about ways to preserve food during the Depression Years, adding another skill for surviving the war years.

    Perhaps the only thing that I recall being missed was sugar and even that was not a problem since we continued to have sweet homemade whipped cream to top hot ginger bread and chocolate syrup seemed to be in plentiful supply for sweetening our milk. Lemonade was plentiful during the summer and I can recall special occasions like that on Pearl Harbor Sunday when we made taffy. Homemade ice cream was cranked out during the hot summer months and there never seemed to any shortages of cookies, fudge or divinity candy during the Christmas holidays. Indeed, the lack of sugar never seemed to be a problem in our family. This was probably due, in part, to the high yields of sugar being shipped in from our Cuban friends to the south, particularly after the U-boat activity ceased to exist in the Florida Straits after the summer of 1942. The supply of candy in stores never seemed to decrease since I remember standing in front of a counter trying to decide which two piece of candy I would buy for one cent, or whether I could splurge with a nickel to buy a whole bag of candy that I could share with my friends. I recall that several of my friends and I would visit the donut shop in Palmetto after basketball practice in 1944 and I recall no limits or restrictions on the number that we could devour as teenagers.

Patriotism was expressed in many ways during those war years. The pledge of allegiance to the flag at school took on new meaning and every kid was somehow involved in the war effort. Balls of string and tinfoil were dropped off in boxes placed in the front hallway of our school and out front was the 20-foot pile where scrap metal was tossed. My brother and I dug out old pipes

Photo 29 - Defense posters reminded citizens to buy US savings stamps and bonds. (*Florida Archives*)

and scraps of metal on the farm and proudly dragged them to the school grounds as part of our commitment to the cause. Individuals and classes were given special awards at the Friday school assemblies for such things as purchases of Saving Stamps and US Savings Bonds.

I remember how enamored I was with the actress

Veronica Lake, who actively participated in patriotic drives throughout Florida. I thought she was the most beautiful thing in the world and as an adolescent dreamed about winning a date with her for saving my pennies to buy US Savings Stamps.

My mother commented once that she thought she would be pretty if she'd "just get that hair out of her eyes." She was particularly active in the Tampa area and I can remember watching a newsreel when she planted a kiss on the cheek of some man who had raised the most money during a Savings Bonds Drive in Hillsborough County. I was an envious teenager.

Photo 30 - Volunteers sign up at the Civic Exhibition Center in St. Petersburg. (*Florida Archives*)

## Jim Wiggins

We carried out buckets of slop from the school cafeteria to feed the "victory pig" out back on the edge of the school property and God help us if we wasted any food. Our principal walked about looking over our shoulders in the cafeteria and we were made to feel that we were depriving our soldiers a meal if we dared to leave anything uneaten on our plates. It was unpatriotic to sharpen our pencils too much, to use a lot of toilet paper, to chew on our erasers, or to throw away the wrappers of our chewing gum without removing the foil. We were reminded by posters to "Zip Your Lips" and not pass along rumors about wartime concerns. We cautioned our parents to slow down while driving, reminding them of Uncle Sam's adage that "Haste is

Photo 31 - Residents of Leesburg proudly display their large pile of scrap metal collected for the war cause. (*Florida Archives*)

Waste," pointing out the learned statistics about the amount of gasoline wasted in speeding.

Shoes and clothing were both rationed, but I imagine that most Floridians never felt the crunch in this area because of the tropical climate. Kids went in their bare feet most of the time and shirts were never worn by boys during the warmer months. I can't ever recall that this was an issue in our home during my teen years and never knew of anyone ever complaining about such. Everyone we knew was pretty much in the same salary bracket and faced the same financial situation as others about them. Clothing simply was never a hardship on anyone I knew and certainly the rationing was no problem for most residents of our Sunshine State. Silk stockings for women seemed to be one of the few clothing shortages ever mentioned since it was still fashionable for women in the '40s to have their legs covered,

Photo 32 - Children proudly display their collection of pots and pans for a scrap metal drive outside the Roxy Theatre in Tampa. (*Florida Archives*)

particularly at church and social functions. For example, my Aunt Mary Louise became quite concerned when she discovered that she had no hose to wear to a fancy faculty reception at the University of Florida where her husband, Vernon Clark, was a law professor. She contacted her sisters and my mother was able ultimately to secure a pair of nylon hose from a friend. My aunt received the hose in the nick of time and all was well. Such a trivial matter was just part of life during those wartime years.

Photo 33 - Students at Florida State College tend their victory garden. (*Florida Archives*)

Naturally, the war became more personal when a loved one was reported missing or dead. Flags were placed in the windows of homes to signify that a member of that particular household was serving their country in one of the Armed Forces. The flag carried a blue star but, sadly, that star was often exchanged for a gold one when a son or husband was killed.

However, many of us were not personally touched by the loss of loved ones in our immediate families and our teenage years were happy and carefree despite the fact that friends and relatives were over there somewhere fighting a war. Indeed, it seemed that kids seemed to build up an immunity to all of the bad stuff that was going on overseas.

Photo 34 - Students and faculty form a "V for Victory" on the campus of the Florida State College in Tallahassee. (*Florida Archives*)

Some of the most traumatic experiences, of course, were shared by wives and girl friends. Take, for example, some of the memories shared by Glorida Condo, girlfriend of my cousin who joined up immediately after graduation from high school. As a teenager growing up in the Morgan family of Plant City where her father was mayor, she recalls many fond memories during the 1940s, including the dances, football and just doing the things that teenagers did in a small town like Plant City. Her recollections about the war years are quite indicative of the commonality shared by many.

## Jim Wiggins

She writes:

*That December of 1941 I was in the 10th grade at Plant City High School, and some of the boys I knew in the upper grades began to enlist. All able-bodied men 18 years and older had to enlist in a service branch or be drafted, although they were allowed to graduate from high school first. In the last part of the war the draft age still began with 18 but had been extended to 40s, but Daddy was just a little older so he didn't have to go.*

*Those Christmases were incredibly poignant. I still can't hear the songs White Christmas, I'll Be Seeing You, I'll Be Home for Christmas, and some of the others popular then without choking up. Every family had a son, husband, brother, or father away from home in military service.*

*All of us grew up fast after the war began. Those of us still in school did volunteer war work to help out on the 'home front.' My sister Panky and I served on a warplane lookout tower on scheduled afternoons, to report by phone and describe to Strategic Air Command headquarters at MacDill Field (in Tampa) every plane that flew over Plant City. Any one of them could have been an enemy plane that sneaked under those early radar systems, as the Japanese at Pearl Harbor did.*

She went on to mention that her boyfriend, my cousin, Kline, did the same thing at Anna Maria Island. The difference was that his lookout was for submarines since it bordered the Gulf of Mexico. She also recalls experiences while visiting at Anna Maria:

*Many ships were sunk close to the beaches, and sometime survivors were picked up in the water by*

> the Coast Guard within sight of swimmers. We saw this happen the summer of '43 while we were vacationing at Anna Maria.

The Beach at the north end of Anna Maria Island was patrolled day and night by bayonet-armed US soldiers who were stationed at the Army radar station on Bean Point at the tip of the island. The Strategic Air Command (SAC) headquarters was located just across Tampa Bay in Tampa and was a prime target too. As the war got worse, Florida's entire coastline was finally under a blackout at night so that targets could not be seen from the air or from enemy submarines.

Gloria writes about how the Red Cross offices were open every day for volunteers to make sterile gauze dressings and to knit wool scarves for military men in cold climates. She and her friends worked on these projects after school and collected scrap metal, rubber and anything that assisted the war effort.

> Instead of saving money in bank accounts, people scrimped and bought War Bonds to help our Government finance the war. Even school children did their part by buying war stamps for 10 cents and saving them in a stamp book until they totaled $18.75, when the book could be exchanged for a $25.00 bond. Care Packages' were sent to loved ones in the service throughout the year, but especially at Christmas. The state Home Demonstration Office would put up food in cans at no charge if it was being sent to servicemen and women, so we saved our sugar ration stamp allotments and baked cookies and other goodies. They stayed fresh for years in those cans. There weren't many gifts that could be used if you were fighting on a Pacific island or European battlefield, but home food was always a welcome treat.

I recall how my own mother baked cookies and, in

particular, fudge that would be boxed and sent to our cousin, DeWayne Condo. My Aunt Myrtle received a letter saying that he and his friends would surely like to have more fudge. My mother had some on the way within days. She made sure that they were thick with pecans.

Gloria and my cousin, Kline, dated during their senior year and he was offered a full football scholarship at the University of Florida. However, he joined the Navy after graduation from high school in 1944 toward the approaching end of the war. She was a student at Florida Southern College at the time and he got only two short leaves during the next three years. They had planned to remain engaged during his time of duty but decided to be married on July 11, 1945, during one of his leaves after he had finished his training in California for the Naval Air Transport Service. They were married in Plant City and my brother, Richard, was best man. They rented a cottage at Anna Maria for their honeymoon but soon Kline departed again, leaving from Tampa back to San Francisco and Honolulu for flight training. He then went on to Guam and spent time in overseas duty with many travels, including trips to China, Japan and the Philippines. By then the war was near its end.

Fortunately, men returning from the military were able to receive an education under the GI Bill. Kline received his degree from the University of Florida where countless other Floridians had already enrolled after their tour of duty. Unlike his brother, he had gone into the service at a rather late date in 1944 and many boys and men had already suffered the consequences of war by this time. Some experienced its horrors with bloodshed and others would simply never return. But for wives like Gloria, the three years of waiting were still long and hard.

Music seemed to take on special importance during the war years, not only in Florida but across the nation. Of course, music always plays an important role in the lives of teenagers and we were no exception despite the fact that extremely serious events were taking place across the oceans. Florida youth, like kids everywhere in the US, tuned in to the Saturday night *Hit Parade* to learn which tunes were rated high on the charts.[5]

The popular songs in the late 1930s were tunes like *Over the Rainbow* and Hoagy Carmichael's *Blue Orchid,* which favored the cherished slow dancing under dimmed lights. Les Brown's *Beer Barrel Polka, Three Little Fishes,* and *Oh, Johnny, Oh Johnny, Oh* illustrate well the levity of the times as society emerged from the Great Depression. The 1940 songs included hits like *The Woodpecker Song, Maybe, Sierra Sue, Blueberry Hill* and Johnny Mercer's *Fools Rush In.* However, by 1941 the music was being greatly influenced by the war. It was that year that *The White Cliffs of Dover* became popular as an expression of concern for our British friends who were facing bombing raids over their cities. Added to that was the song, *'Til Reveille* which acknowledged the rapidly growing number of recruits who were facing reveille in the military barracks.

This did not mean that the music industry was in any way constrained by the existence of war. Rather, it seemed almost as though comical relief was a necessary part of surviving the times. Many songs were silly and lighthearted, perhaps serving as a catharsis to relieve the anxieties being brought on by war. Tunes such as *The Hut Sut Song* and *Chattanooga Choo Choo* did just that. Even the event of Pearl Harbor and the declaration of war by Congress did not seem to deter the interest in frivolous songs such as those which hit the top of the charts in 1941. *Deep in the Heart of Texas, Jingle, Jingle, Jingle* and *I've Got a Gal in Kalamazoo* were on the lips of youth everywhere. 1942 had military themes which included *He Wears a Pair of Silver Wings* and *Don't Sit Under the Apple Tree,* the plea of a serviceman asking that his girl friend not sit under the apple tree with anyone else until he came marching home. (A citrus tree would have been more appropriate

## Jim Wiggins

for Floridians.)

*Praise the Lord and Pass the Ammunition* was being sung everywhere in 1942 and it was one of those tunes that was being hummed by everyone in the streets and at the work place. In fact, it was just one of those tunes that just wouldn't go away. Interestingly enough, few people raised the question about whether this song was politically or morally correct. Supposedly, the inspiration for the song originated with a chaplain who was serving duty on the front lines. Irving Berlin's *I Left My Heart at the Stage Door Canteen* was introduced in the musical theatre, *This Is The Army,* as was Johnny Mercer's *The Fleet's In*. *When the Lights Go on Again* expressed the wishful thinking of the public for a time when bombings and blackouts would be no more.

The year 1943 had many hit records from bands such as Xavier Cugat and Jimmy Dorsey. Catchy tunes such as *Elmer's Tune* were played everywhere but one of the heart-wrenching songs was *Comin' In on a Wing and a Prayer*, made particularly poignant by the increased number of US aviators who were losing their lives while on bombing missions. *I'll be Home for Christmas* hit the top on charts in 1944 as favorable war news brought hope for the return of loved ones before the holidays. Cole Porter's *Don't Fence Me In* and Johnny Burke's *Swinging on a Star* were top favorites. That year also featured Johnny Mercer's *Accentuate the Positive* and saw Les Brown's *Sentimental Journey* rise to the top of the charts. Oscar Hammerstein's musical film, *State Fair,* expressed levity and joy in *It MightaAs Well be Spring*, a sense of a new beginning as the war came to an end.

The listing of these songs during the years of World War II helps to illustrate the manner in which life went on even though a war was being fought somewhere else. Despite the absence of loved ones and the signs of war in every storefront and on every corner, life did move on. Team sports, teen proms, cruising the drive-ins and jitterbugging were all a part of youthful activities.

## Jim Wiggins

Competitive sports continued as teams managed to find ways to travel distances to play their rivals. Parents and friends pitched in their ration cards to insure gas for buses and trucks left school parking lots loaded down with passengers crowded together to conserve use of gasoline and the wear on tires. My own father, for example, always went to the gym parking lot to offer rides to those who could not otherwise attend the out-of-town school games. Many of the seniors, of course, were anxiously awaiting graduation in order to sign up for military and all the friends cherished their last periods of time together.

Most family activities in Florida during the summer time centered around the water and our family was no exception. We gathered scallops on the shallow grassy flats on the edge of Tampa Bay, dug clams and scrounged the bayous for mullet to be caught in cast nets. We spent evenings with our friends stationed like sentries with our 12 foot, seven- pronged gigs waiting for the shadow of a snook to pass under the Anna Maria pier. My brother and I made much of our spending money selling speckled trout caught within 100 yards of the pier and at night we would wade with our homemade ice-pick gigs to spear flounders that would be tossed into floating washtubs. Mangrove snapper were readily caught on changing tides under the pier and there was never any shortage of fresh fish on the dinner table.

Our family owned a small cottage at Anna Maria Island for several years at a time when the war was at its height. I worked a couple of summers on the pier catching and selling bait, renting poles and squeezing lemonade at a time when a Coast Guard cruiser was tied up alongside, a constant reminder that we were at war. We watched US aircraft strafing a nearby island in target practice and, on one occasion, watched with horror when the pilot failed to pull out. The Coast Guard cutter rushed to the scene and returned to the pier with the body of the pilot distributed in wire baskets used for such a grim procedure.

## Jim Wiggins

One of the young crewman, a fellow from Brooklyn named Mike, became a friend and delighted in joining us for dinner at our home. He relished eating mangoes, a delicacy introduced to him for the first time during that summer of 1943. The presence of a Coast Guard cutter and its crewmen in our midst was just part of the total package, as was the continued surveillance from patrol towers on the beach and requirements for blackout curtains after dark.

With the exception of the German U-boat activity in Florida waters during 1942, there never seemed to be a sense of fear among Floridians for their own personal safety. At least, this was my perception as a teenager. True, there were the sporadic periods of blackouts and the patrolling of beaches, but there was no sense of a prevailing threat from the enemy. The reality of war was somewhere else across the wide expanse of oceans and we felt far removed except for the consequences of having loved ones and friends involved in those places about which we knew little.

However, there was often an underlying sense of foreboding that hovered over the citizenry. I recall once hearing the approach of a squadron of B-12s moving south overhead from MacDill Air Field and thinking to myself as I saw them come into view, "Now what if that were a squadron of German warplanes? What would we do?" It was with a sense of awe that we watched such squadrons fly overhead but at the same time it was not unusual to allow our imagination to work overtime. After all, there was a lot of propaganda being disseminated by the government and we were constantly being reminded to be alert. Adults, quite naturally, understood better the consequences of war but there is no doubt that children and young people also absorbed much of the existing anxiety.

Take, for example, the Sniff Kit. "The Sniff Kit?" one asks. "What in the world was that?" The Sniff Kit was a kit that was approved and recommended by the Office of Civilian Defense and the Chemical Warfare Service of the US Army. Our school had one. It sat up high on a shelf in the corner of the principal's room where our seventh- and eighth-grade classes met. Our principal, Mrs. Buena Lee Meade, explained briefly what it was but did not dwell on it, nor did she demonstrate how it was used. Obviously, it was simply one of those things recommended to be made available to every school faculty in case of an emergency.

The Sniff Kit was designed to provide an easy and safe method of identifying the five principal gases used in chemical warfare. The outer case was made of wood and pressboard, covered with a tan saddle fabric. It contained five bottles with

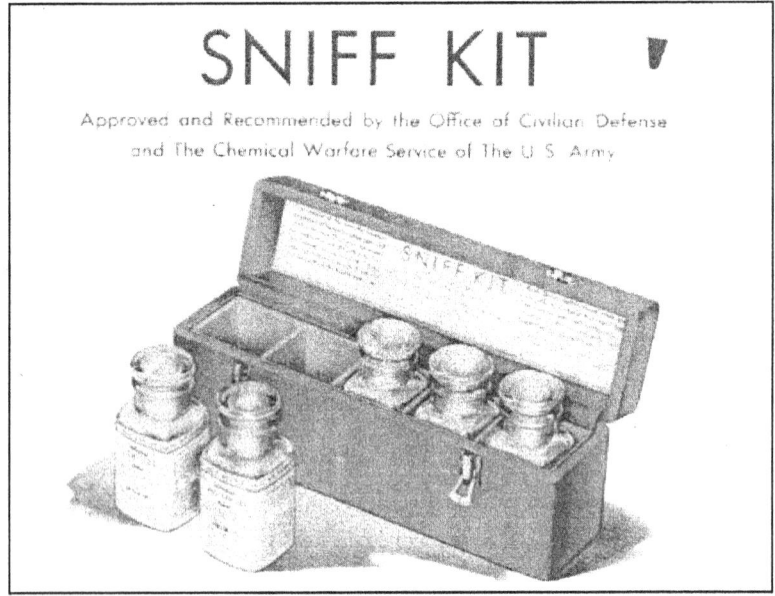

Photo 35 - Sniff Kits were distributed throughout Florida schools by the US Army to make students aware of possible enemy threats with the use of chemical warfare. (*Florida Archives*)

ground glass stoppers, charged with the following imitations: mustard gas (HS), phosgene gas (CG), chloricrin (PS), lewisite (MI or M-1) and teargas (CN). Each bottle was labeled with simple information that described the physiological effect of the active gas and gave instructions for treating victims. The life of these imitations was guaranteed for not less than four months of normal use, provided that the bottles were kept tightly closed when not in use. The kits sold for $5 each. The presence of these kits in schools and elsewhere illustrates well the unknown possibilities and fears inherent through war. I cannot recall that any of us kids ever gave the kit much consideration. However, the fact that I still can picture it on a shelf must indicate that it did make an impact on our young impressionable minds.

Again, there were never any direct land attacks by Axis powers on American soil but Floridians, in particular, felt vulnerable after viewing the German U-boat activity so close by. Even before the bombing of Pearl Harbor there was a sense of vulnerability by many Floridians. Some citizens were concerned enough to take action. In August of 1940 Mr. Guy Allen of Tampa was instrumental in setting up an unofficial "Florida Motorcycle Corps" to help patrol beach areas for possible attacks from German submarines. This Motorcycle Corps later became part of the State Defense Council, which was set up in early 1941 by the Florida Legislature. By that time the original motorcycle group was being used to escort military convoys.

Of course, each particular area in Florida had its own distinctive involvement on the home front during the war. Some communities were on the edge of bombing ranges and had to endure explosions and rattling windows. Some areas encountered incessant convoys of trucks while others lived under the fly zones of air bases. Fishermen were prohibited in waters such as Florida Bay where bombs targeted shallow reefs and no one was allowed to build bonfires and party on the beaches. Indeed, only residents with identification were allowed to cross over bridges to waterfront homes in such places as Palm Beach and other island communities along the eastern coastline and soldiers were stationed at checkpoints on bridges to check credentials. Each location seemed to share in their own particular and unique experiences, depending entirely on the nature of the nearby military operations.

Take, for example, Miami Beach. There was almost hysteria when German submarines were sighted off Florida's beaches on the east coast and the Army Air Corps responded immediately when a U-boat sank *Pan Massachusetts* in February of 1942, announcing that it would be moving into Miami Beach to begin training on the very next day. Tourists were given only 24 hours to move out of hotels and 500 men showed up the next night to move into five hotels at a rented price of $10 per man per

Photo 36 - Truck convoys traveled regularly on Florida highways. This convoy from Camp Blanding was waiting to load soldiers. (*Florida Archives*)

month. Within three months, the military had taken over 70,000 rooms, which were 85 percent of all the hotels in Miami Beach. The young recruits usually bunked two to four men to a room but no one complained about their accommodations.

## Jim Wiggins

    Miami Beach became one of the world's most unusual boot camps. Men from out of state did complain about the heat and getting sand in their boots but, for the most part, they were happy to be in a tropical paradise. They were allowed to do calisthenics in shorts or bathing suits and took dips in the ocean after drills and marches. Their food was served in some of Miami's best cafeterias and restaurants. One soldier wrote, "Dear Mom, the army sure has gone swell all of a sudden, and it's just like the travel folders say."[6] German and Italian prisoners were also brought in daily from a camp in southwest Miami to work detail on the beach. Some girls who exercised at a nearby junior high school gym class observed the prisoners at work and one made the following observation, "They worked with their shirts off, and some of them were so handsome. I didn't know whether to hate them or swoon over them."[7]

    Amazingly, tourists continued to pour into Miami Beach during the war in spite of gas and tire rationing. Housing was short and the families of enlisted men found it difficult to find anything to rent. Prices were high and, in time, tourists were encouraged to stay away. However, parties flourished and money flowed freely despite the fact that the GI's budget was only $50 per month. The most popular drink for servicemen was the "B-29," consisting of rye, bourbon or gin, passion fruit, pineapple and lime. Miami Beach's theme song was *Rum and Coca Cola* since it was said to be drunk by most everyone. The home front in Miami and Miami Beach, like most places in Florida, had its own unique war history.

## Jim Wiggins

In May of 1942, 1,200 men were moved into the plush Boca Raton Club where they were to be trained by the Army Air Force. The Breakers Hotel in Palm Beach housed the wounded; The Hollywood Beach Hotel hosted a naval training school; the Ponce de Leon Hotel in St. Augustine became a coast guard center; and more than 10,000 servicemen moved into men's

Photo 37 - Servicemen gather at the USO in Jacksonville. (*Florida Archives*)

dormitories at university campuses. Hotels throughout Florida were converted into military installations and restaurants rapidly became mess halls. No area in Florida was immune to these overnight changes.

The citrus and vegetable industry grew by leaps and bounds. The US government requisitioned all canned and processed fruits between the years of 1942 to 1945 for the military and lend-lease purposes. Farm workers were imported from the Bahamas, Jamaica and Barbados to join in with Italian and German POWs to harvest Florida's crops. Prisoners were transported by bus where sugar cane was harvested and where citrus crops needed to be picked. In Lee County, 700 men from Buckingham Army Air Field volunteered to work on their three-day monthly leave to harvest potatoes that would have otherwise perished due to the lack of available laborers. Employment in Florida was at an all-time high and there were labor shortages everywhere.

Photo 38 - USO activities for servicemen at Tallahassee included dances and outings. (*Florida Archives*)

    Labor shortages were demonstrated in my own hometown by the fact that teenagers were employed for jobs normally filled by adults. Indeed, as stated by Gloria Condo, all of us had to grow up quickly since so much more was required of us than in previous generations. Jobs were waiting to be filled. Some required immediate attention. For example, at age 13 I was issued my first Social Security Card and was hired at the local tomato cannery. My older brother, cousins and friends were all employed. After all, ripe tomatoes rot quickly and timing was all-important if the crops were to be salvaged. (The choice green tomatoes had already been picked and shipped north.) Donna (Holly) Simpson, a cousin, recalls those years: "During the war, schools structured their terms so that students might help harvest the local tomato crops. I worked in a packing house, grading tomatoes. We were all so tired, but felt like we were doing our part for the war effort."

Teenage girls and women stood at the conveyor belts and culled tomatoes. I helped unload tomatoes brought in by trucks and dumped them onto the waiting belts. My brother, Richard, and his older friends worked longer hours, doing important jobs such as processing the tomato juice in huge steaming vats, canning, or stacking the finished product for transportation onto waiting trucks. All of the tomato packing houses across Florida were crowded with seasonal teenage and women workers who filled jobs previously held by men. It offered teenagers a rare chance to make money and, admittedly, our employers could not be too picky in their selection of workers, a fact that assured everyone a chance at seasonal work.

Those of us on the home front just kept doing our thing but it must be remembered that everything was done within the context of patriotism and with a sense that every action be evaluated in terms of what contributed best to the war effort. This did not mean that frivolous activity was frowned upon. Indeed, the opposite appeared to be true. We were not embedded in a cocoon of seriousness but, rather, teenagers were carefree and somewhat reckless, illustrated well by the popular music listed beforehand that lent to the enjoyment of jitterbugging and boisterous activity. Our focus as teenagers was not on the war itself but, rather, on the daily events of each new day that involved routine peer pressure and meeting the obligations expected of us as students and family members. There was nothing complicated about living through those war years except, perhaps, we did have to grow up a little faster, particularly young men right out of high school who immediately faced induction into military service. It

## Jim Wiggins

was simply all that we knew. The economy in Florida was at an all-time high and we stood on the edge of a changing society unlike any that our state had ever known.

Life was good. The war came and went. We were part of it, perhaps absorbed in it to such a degree that it almost came and went without being noticed for the enormous impact it made upon our lives. But for those whose sacrifice meant the loss of loved ones, it would leave an indelible void that could never be healed. Two hundred fifty thousand Floridians served in the armed forces during the war but that number represents only a small percentage of those whose lives were forever changed because of it. Indeed, every single person living within the Sunshine State during those formative years will forever bear an indelible stamp upon our memories that can never be erased with the passage of time.

# Chapter Nine

# They Remember

My father's cousin, Earl Hardin, was among those reported missing in action.[1] The telegram to his wife, Jewel,

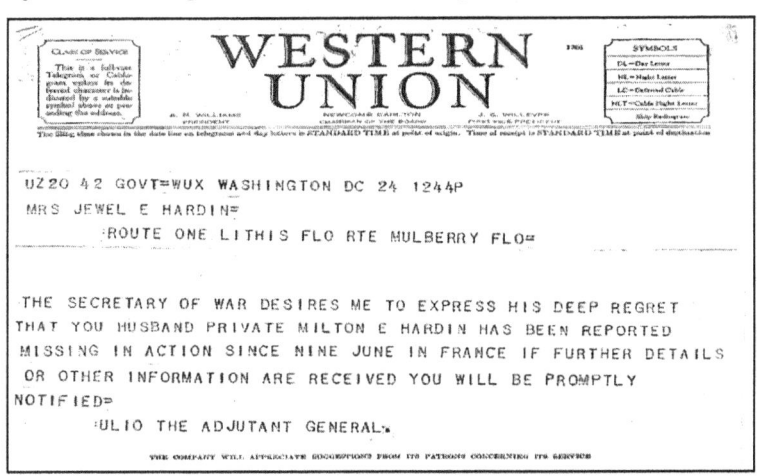

Photo 39 – Telegram from War Department. (*Jewel Hardin*)

arrived on the day before Christmas, declaring that he had been missing since June 9. Fortunately, in the case of Earl, a second

## Jim Wiggins

telegram was received to inform Jewel that the International Red Cross had discovered that he was a German prisoner of war. Later, a letter written with a pencil on V-mail paper that carried no date, stamp, or postmark, arrived from Earl, stating that he had escaped. It read:

> *I got away from the Jerries in February and have been on the front line with the Russian $1^{st}$ army.*

Photo 40 - Milton Earl Hardin of Ellenton, Florida, was reported missing in action before his daring escape from a German prison camp. (*Jewel Hardin*)

> *Had lots of luck up until the next to the last day. I got it in the foot. I think the Russians are the best guys I have ever met. They will give you anything they have or go in and get it for you. I would like to tell you of the things I saw in Berlin and some of the towns I have been to. Everything you have read in the papers about their camps over here...well, they are about five times that bad. When I ran away (escaped from the Germans) I was down to 127 pounds but the Russians got me back on my feet. (His wife said he weighed 188 pounds when he went into active duty with Company "L" of Palmetto.)*

Thankfully, unlike many other wives, Jewel didn't have to

## Jim Wiggins

put a gold star in her window since Earl returned home all safe and sound, ready and raring to use his expertise as one of the community's best throwers of a castnet, soon spreading it wide over schools of mullet that he was stalking as he always did before. But like all other prisoners of war, he held special memories of war's worst experiences. Those memories were later recorded. The following account is unusually graphic and for this reason it is printed in its entirety.

>   *Hi, my name is M. Earl Hardin.* [2] *I will attempt to tell my entire World War II experience as a German prisoner of war and later as a Russian soldier fighting the Germans. After my basic training we were all assigned to various units for further training. Somehow, I ended up at Ft. Benning, Ga. My job there was to assist the officer instructor at the machine gun school. We had to set up the guns and fire at various targets as demonstrations of a machine gun in combat. Later, I was assigned to l. Co., 3rd Bn., 8th Inf. 4th Div., and went over to England with them. There we got a lot more training and practiced landing on the beaches at a place called Slapton Sands. We knew that the invasion was coming soon, but none of us knew when or where until the last minute. For want of a better word, I'll just say we were concerned, because we knew some of us would not make it back and there would be wounded. Our officers tried to keep us busy, cleaning weapons and going over last minute details. I think they were just as scared as we were, but tried to keep it hidden.*

>   *The channel crossing was very rough. Many of us got seasick and had to heave our guts out. The tension we all felt certainly didn't help. When we went over the side into the landing craft, I began to*

## Jim Wiggins

*feel better because I saw General Teddy Roosevelt was in our boat.[3] His calm, almost cheery attitude seemed to settle everyone down. According to the General, we were very lucky because we landed on the wrong beach and met only light resistance. I don't remember much about the next few days. I know our company joined in the attack inland almost immediately. As enlisted men, we didn't have maps and were unable to read French. I just don't recall any of the small towns we captured. Our casualties were very light and I recall thinking this was going to be easy to lick the Germans.*

*I was now a Buck Sergeant and Assistant Squad Leader. On June 10th, I was sent out to establish a machine gun position in front of our company. Somehow, we got lost near a small airfield. One small plane hangar there looked deserted, so we went to check it out. It was empty, but just beyond it we saw some open trenches which looked abandoned. They offered us some cover to cross the field, so we got in them and started across. We had gone about 100 yards from the hangar, when suddenly we were confronted by a large group of Germans. They fired on us and I was hit in the legs, so we quickly surrendered. They allowed me to put sulfur powder on my slight flesh wound and bandaged it up. Damn! I thought as we were marched off. Only the 4th day of the war and it was already over for me! I really had no idea how little I knew of what might lie ahead.*

*Stripped of our weapons, we were herded like sheep toward the German rear. Our small group grew as more POWs from the 82nd and 101st airborne were added several times. We were not allowed to talk and could only guess what our guards were thinking. The roads were jammed with*

## Jim Wiggins

*German troops and equipment, as I suppose various units were being moved to their newly assigned positions. Also, added to the confusion, were ambulances and other vehicles headed to the rear. I suppose some were going back for more ammo. Allied planes caused us to scatter several times as they came along to strafe the roadway. They really created havoc, as they left behind burning vehicles and the dead and wounded. A couple of our POWs got hit, but we were unable to help. I don't know how badly they were wounded or if they were killed. Our capture took place about 10 a.m. We were on the road all day and all night. About daylight on June 11th, we reached St. Lo, having marched over 30 miles.*

*The Germans did not attempt to interview us. Perhaps they thought the enlisted men didn't know enough to bother with us. However, they did interview the officers. We were told we had to work under rules of the Geneva Convention. I was assigned to do work at the hospital there. Our job was to carry in the wounded from the ambulances. Some of the wounded were really torn to pieces. Apparently, this hospital was a forward field hospital because some of the wounded were patched up and we carried them back out to other ambulances which took them farther to the rear. Still others didn't make it and we carried them out to the meat wagon. I don't know where they were taken for burial.*

*Next, we were moved to Chartres where we again worked at a hospital doing the same thing. Our move from St. Lo to Chartres was by truck. I think we were in Chartres about four days when we were moved again by truck to the vicinity of Paris.*

## Jim Wiggins

*At Paris our work was all manual labor. The Germans were very anxious to clean up the bombed out railroads. We had to move a lot of wreckage, old tracks, ties, etc. The guards really worked us hard here. I was glad my leg had almost healed up; thanks to the sulfur powder. I was grateful it had not been a serious wound. Once we had cleaned up most of the debris, the German crews came in to lay new track. No longer needed here, we moved again. This time by rail in 40 and 8 (40 men or 8 horses) box cars. Allied planes again shot us up and knocked out the engine. We were stuck there until another engine could be brought to help us. It took several days to make it to Cologne, our next stop. I'm not sure of the name of this stalag, but I think it was Belsen. From small windows in our stalag, where we were locked in every night, we could hear the bombing of Cologne and see the flashes and later fires caused by the bombs. It was eerie to know what these bombs were doing to the city of Cologne. I got a first hand view of the terrible destruction caused by the severe bombing on July 4th.*

*Some of our men had to work in a nearby coal mine, but I was assigned to a large detail of men sent into Cologne to clean up the rubble. Our main job was to clear the roads and work in some warehouse areas. We did find a few bodies under the debris. We saw first hand how much destruction bombs can cause. It did not make us feel sorry for the Germans because they had started this terrible war and Hitler did not hesitate to bomb Poland, Russia and England without mercy. All of us, in one way or another, expressed our gratitude that this destruction was not hitting home in America.*

## Jim Wiggins

*As the American armies moved across France in late August, we were moved by rail to Dachau. This was 15 or 20 miles from Munich. Near where we got off the train, I saw my first real evidence of German atrocities. Dead bodies of bullet-riddled men hung in and on the barbed wire fence around the stockade. They apparently had been left to remind all that attempted escape; it was very dangerous. I had heard the Germans were killing a lot of Jews and this seemed to bear this out. We could see long rows across the field of fresh dirt that could have been graves and the gas chambers and incinerators behind them. At that time, we were not aware what they were, but found out when I went there for a visit a few years ago. They must have been in use then because the stench was terrible. I cannot believe that anyone could live in the area and not know that mass killings were going on here. Train after train came in loaded with Jews and pulled away empty. Every day I thought about escaping, but the bodies on the fence made you realize how foolish it would be to try. I tried to blot out thinking about my wife and home. It was hard to keep telling yourself that they were okay.*

*Our food was terrible. Perhaps you think you wouldn't eat garbage, or rats, horsemeat, or half rotten food. Most normal men wouldn't but I have seen men fight each other over a small portion. After a while you almost cease to exist as man and become more and more like a beast. Human dignity, honest and fair play are almost constant internal battles. Many men break down under the physical and emotional strain. When your physical condition runs down, it seems harder to control your emotions. Even a letter from home could mean so very much. You could read it over and over.*

## Jim Wiggins

*Mail was very rare and then only because of the help of the Red Cross. Without the Red Cross parcels, many of us would not have made it.*

*My next stalag was near Berlin called Buchenwald. We were moved here in mid Sept. '44. Various work details were again assigned. My buddy from I Company, Bill Shimaki V, [4] and I volunteered to work in construction of a new cafeteria. We were to work with a couple of older Germans who were stone and brick masons. This sounded like a good deal to us and the thought entered my head that it might be easier to escape from a smaller group.*

*Our job was to mix cement and keep the two masons busy by supplying all the mud and bricks the men would need. One of the men spoke English quite well and he asked all kinds of questions. They were not about the war so it was easy to talk with him. One day he asked me how I thought the war was going. I told him frankly that it was easy to see the Germans were losing. They were being pushed back on every front. The Americans and British were now on their west border and Russia was almost at the Polish border. It won't be long now and Germany will lose. He told me many Germans now felt the same way.*

*Somehow, I got up the nerve to tell him that Bill and I would really like to escape. He stopped, looked me in the eye and asked for a cigarette. Over our smoke he wanted to know if I had very many cigarettes. I told him we had a few packs. Then he said, 'If you can come up with about 10 packs, I could help you escape.' I asked him how, and he replied, 'through the underground. That's all I can tell you now.'*

## Jim Wiggins

*Well, Bill and I went to work on getting 10 packs. Some men didn't smoke, so we went to work on them. We traded off every souvenir we had and after about two weeks, we had 10 packs. A couple of days later, he proved his word was good and led us to a small town called Cotlbus. There we met two older men from the German underground. They told us they could get us out, but it would be into Poland. They didn't have any contacts to the West or South. At this point, we didn't want to go back to a POW camp so we decided to go to Poland. Bill and I were both very ignorant of some of the facts, which should have been obvious. Poland was a bitter enemy of both Germany and Russia. This was now October and the heavy Polish winter would soon be here. Food would be very scarce in Poland since she had been ravaged by both armies. The Russians would soon be fighting Poland and we would have to hide from the Germans and maybe even the Russians. Our present freedom blinded us to the storms ahead. Without hesitation, we followed our German underground guides into Poland. All the German guides were at least 60 or older. I'm sure they felt some good might come to them for helping us. I doubt that it helped them, but it sure helped us get out of Germany.*

*Now our Polish guides led us deeper into Poland. They felt, and we agreed, that the Russians were better German enemies and we would be better off if we could get through and behind the Russians. Our food was so very scarce, I thought we might starve. Both German and Polish guides had shown us how to salvage some food. When we could find old earthen food cellars, we usually managed to get something. Sometimes we found carrots, turnips, sugar beets, parsnips and potatoes. The Polish*

## Jim Wiggins

*people helped us when they could. In desperation, we even sneaked into a German convoy and stole a few rations. Sometimes, we found caches of food that had been hidden for us. Because of the deep snow and cold, every day was sheer misery.*

*Somehow, we managed in about three months to walk over 800 miles. We either by-passed or stuck to the outskirts of the bigger towns like Poznan and Warsaw. Our guides decided there would be heavy fighting between the partisans and Germans in Warsaw and guided us on to Brest. It was tricky coming up to the rear of the main German line and then sneaking on through it and the Russian front line. Our guides were very good and knew that part of the country very well. Otherwise, I doubt we would have been so lucky. Once into the Russian lines, they contacted a Russian officer who took us to headquarters. Unable to speak or understand either language, we were strictly at their mercy.*

*Finally, we were told that we would have to fight for the Russian army if we wanted to be fed. Very hungry, we agreed that eating regular meals again would be worth it, so we agreed to fight. However, to do this, we would still have to march another 150 miles to join up with a tank outfit to our North where they had an English-speaking officer. This was now late December in 1944 and the weather was very cold. Our guides were usually able to find some type of shelter to sleep in. Frequently, in old sheds or barns where we could find some hay to sleep on. It was a great comfort to find some hay since we didn't have enough blankets, but only the clothes we wore and our coats. Our constant hunger was the biggest problem. We really needed some meat but it was very scarce. A couple of times some nice Polish people gave us some eggs and*

## Jim Wiggins

*once we had a chicken. It was just great to get the extra food. We made a feast out of it.*

*The farther we marched into Poland the more I became concerned about our decision. I don't see how we could have been worse off as German prisoners. Sure, the food had been terrible and we had to work, but at least we had a building and bunk to sleep in. It didn't pay to worry about it because there was no way we could turn back now.*

*In mid-January, we finally caught up with the Russian tank outfit. We had been in hiding and on the road for about 3 1/2 months. We looked and felt like a couple of hobos. Our number one problem was food and the guides told us the Russian would feed us. They took us to the tank commander, a Lt. Fisher who spoke excellent English. He had graduated from Harvard, we were told. We were questioned at length about our imprisonment and our combat experience. Lt. Fisher then told us he was authorized to feed only the soldiers under his command. He said, 'If you want to eat, you will have to join the Russian army.' Bill and I were so hungry, we did not hesitate and joined the Russian army in ex officio capacity. Quite a few Poles had joined in the same way. We received no pay and were never issued serial numbers. Therefore, if we had been killed, no one would ever know.*

*I asked Lt. Fisher what would happen to us if we got wounded. He replied, 'It all depends. If you get a serious wound, the Russian army has no way to take care of their seriously wounded men. If you lose an arm or leg or get a severe gut wound, you will be left to survive, if you can. If your wound is such that you will recover to fight again, our medics will treat you quickly the best they can and you will* be evacuated if necessary.' This became a constant worry. We knew that if we were seriously wounded, we would be abandoned and would surely die.

Our tank unit was near the town of Bialystok, not far from the Baltic. We were part of the $2^{nd}$ White Russian Army. We did not advance for a few weeks as the army brought up supplies for the next stage of battle. This gave us a little break we much needed.

I don't know how to describe the whole army unit. Lt. Fisher seemed to be in charge of about 12 tanks and crew, plus the infantry that worked with the tanks.

Lt. Fisher was from Romania and fled to Moscow with his wife when the Germans overran Romania. In Moscow, they both joined the Red Army. Because of his education, he was made an officer and sent to a quick school to learn about tanks. His wife, Gracie, was trained as a tank driver. Three other women in the outfit were also tank drivers. They were all very good drivers. Later, two of them got killed when their tanks got hit.

In the rear of our army, several thousand women and children followed the troops everywhere. At night the women came up to comfort the men and to salvage any food they could for themselves and their children. These tough Russian women lived in the worst possible conditions, yet they did more than keep up with the army. They helped dig trenches, carry supplies, take care of the wounded, endured shelling and froze in the deep snow and cold. No one has any idea how many of these women and children perished from the war from lack of food and from the terrible cold. The losses had to be very severe based on what the army had to endure.

## Jim Wiggins

*The tank crews and support infantry mostly came from the cities and so were probably better educated than a large block of the Russian army. I suppose the unit I fought with was similar to many other tank units. When in the attack there seemed to be at least a platoon of infantrymen on the ground around us and some riding on each tank. We used the tanks as shields when we could and hid behind them to protect us from shelling and small arms fire. Our tanks never advanced without the infantry. Many times, we were ordered to advance straight into the German lines. This caused many casualties but the men seemed very willing to attack in this manner. They were so determined to get to Berlin that no amount of losses seemed to stop them they fought like savages. When small groups of Germans, such as a machine gun nest surrendered, they were all shot. Very few prisoners were taken. They all seemed to remember some German atrocity...some villages that had been burned, some civilian hung or shot by firing squads, some heads bashed in, women raped. It's hard to describe the hatred.*

*Once I saw a Russian Captain go in a house where a young mother (probably Polish) was changing her baby. Some older folks were standing in the background looking very frightened. The Captain grabbed the baby by the heels and threw it head first on the floor and then stomped the baby's head crushing it. He then shot the three innocent civilians. I was told this sort of thing happened many times. The Captain had lost his entire family in a similar manner. The Russians seemed to hate the Poles as much as the Germans.*

*It was my observation that the Russians deliberately delayed going into Warsaw to help the*

## Jim Wiggins

Poles when some 300,000 Poles under General Bor rose up to fight the Germans there. Finally, when the Germans had defeated the Poles and massacred them by the thousands, the Russian army advanced and took Warsaw.

As our army began to advance, we found out how tough it is to fight in winter. At times, snowdrifts were as high as the turret of the tank. Often snow was three feet deep. Many of our vehicles got stuck and it was difficult to get them out. Sometimes we rode the tanks, but it was so cold most of the time we walked behind in the tank tracks. Sometimes it got warm walking with our heavy winter clothes and heavy coats, so we tied our coats on the tank and hoped to catch it again before it got too cold.

The Germans were fierce fighters, especially the closer we got to Germany. I think the only way we could defeat them now was because at this stage of the war the Russian air force was far superior to that of the Germans. The Germans had lost so many planes that they were no match for the Russian fighter planes. I'm also sure that Hitler weakened the entire eastern front to gather additional strength for his Battle of the Bulge. We were also able to surround thousands of Germans because Hitler would not let them withdraw to a better defense position.

It was difficult for Bill and I to fight as infantry. We could not understand the orders given us by the infantry officers and we had to more or less follow the other men and try to do as they were doing.

In the last village we had taken, I walked into a building and saw a German lying on the floor. I thought he was dead and turned to walk out when he jumped up and lunged at me with a bayonet. I *heard him just in time to save my life and turned sideways, thus avoiding his main thrust. He still cut into my shoulder but I was able to kill him before he could make another thrust. Then a woman behind him rushed me with a knife and I had to kill her. I don't know what he meant to her for this was still in Poland.*

*Because of my slight wound and other problems, I decided to talk with Lt. Fisher. In talking to Lt. Fisher about these problems, he asked if we could drive a truck. When assured that we could, he assigned us as truck drivers. This probably saved our lives because in the next attack our unit's losses were very severe and several of our tanks were knocked out. As truck drivers we hauled ammo, gas, food, and any other supplies our unit needed. A Russian always went with us and carried the orders for supplies. This was a much safer, though very difficult job. Sometimes, German fighters came down to strafe us and we were shelled many times. The roads were very rough, often packed with snow and ice. It would have been easy to smash up the truck with its dangerous cargo. Sometimes we had to travel over a hundred miles to the supply dumps. Our American made 2 1/2 ton 6x6 GMC truck was very rugged and we made it through some almost impassable roads. Sometimes we had to be very careful to avoid big shell holes in the road, especially at night. When the situation demanded it, we sometimes drove night and day for a few days.*

*As near as I can remember, we were somewhere near Poznan and seemed to be building up supplies, especially artillery ammo, for the last big drive on to Berlin. We had heard rumors that the Americans were attacking into Czechoslovakia. Bill and I were very apprehensive about fighting with the Russians in taking Berlin. We felt sure the Germans would put up a very stiff fight and knew how determined the Russians were to take it. Because of our truck driving, we had maps and it didn't look very far to Prague.*

*Having decided to escape, we carefully made our plans. It was easy to get gas, rifle ammo, grenades and food at supply without anyone taking notice. On the day selected, we asked our Russian guides to go with us, but when they declined we shot them and then took off in my truck. Since we were traveling across the rear of our army most of the way it was easy to get through the various checkpoints by just holding up our orders. However, as we passed into another Russian army zone, it was more difficult. A couple of times we had to shoot our way through. I think we shot 12 or 13 Russian guards altogether. Fighting was still going on in Prague, so we bypassed it and went on to the vicinity of Pilsen where we were finally lucky enough to find some American infantry from, I believe, the 16th Division.*

*After some interrogation, we were taken to an army hospital where we were fed, given complete physicals and kept for observation. Our Russian food had helped restore our health, we were soon released, and after some of the red tape was checked out, we were told we would soon be on our way home. Army records caught up and we were paid for all the months we had been listed as POWs. Over 10 months as POWs and Russian soldiers.*

*It was my observation that it was much tougher to be a Russian soldier than a POW. My American army experience was so brief that I have almost forgotten what it was like. I believe the Americans were better trained than the Russians, but because of their hatred of the Germans, they were probably tougher, better fighters. Most of the Russian equipment was American made so the two armies were very much alike here. I think the Russians were more inclined to sacrifice men and material to win a battle. The Russian soldier was better equipped in winter clothes than either the Germans or the Americans and that was a very important part of winning the war. I'm sure with proper clothing many Americans would have withstood the rigors of the Russian front. After all, Bill and I made it. Thank God.*[5]

Earl's mother lived in her big sprawling home, which was only two houses down the road from us. Aunt Mae and Earl's wife, Jewel, joyously welcomed him home and the stories about his war experiences were soon circulating throughout the community. Having been a prisoner of war made him an extraordinary hero. Indeed, his stories made our hair stand on end and we couldn't get enough of them. The above account, however, was not released until years later and shows just how harsh war can be.

Many other local servicemen, including two other cousins, DeWayne Condo (who lived next door) and Wallace Wood, also returned home and shared many horror stories about combat duty. They remembered, but their stories never quite measured up to Earl's tales that particularly intrigued all of us teenagers who enjoyed hearing of daring exploits of escapes and killings. DeWayne and Wallace, however, certainly caught the community's attention by flying low over our homes in small planes that were rented at the Sarasota airport. Our houses would actually shake when they flew low wagging their wings. These two ex-pilots also enjoyed "dogfights" over the Manatee River. My mother used to complain that one of them was going to end of killing himself with "all of that showing off." Sure enough, Wallace was later killed in Texas flying low in a duster plane while showing off for his wife.

Most men and women who served in the US armed services during World War II never recorded their experiences. This, of course, is a shame. Indeed, the experiences were so

Photo 41 - Captain Colin P. Kelly, Jr., of Madison, Florida, was credited with being the first US war hero. (*Florida Archives*)

traumatic for some that they could never talk about them. This was understandable since post-war stress was common. Many, like Earl, later revisited the sites where they served and relived their experiences. Unfortunately, only a small percentage bothered to

## Jim Wiggins

put their experiences in writing. Thankfully, Earl Hardin saw fit to share his memories and, as a result, left a legacy that will forever live on.[6]

Some Florida men would not return home to share their memories. Captain Colin P. Kelly, Jr. was one of those men. Kelly was credited with being America's first hero of World War II by attacking and sinking the Japanese battleship, *Haruna,* off Luzon in the Philippines on December 10, 1941. His B-17 was shot while returning to its base and burst into flames. His waist gunner was killed but Kelly ordered the rest of the crew to bail out. Captain Kelly, however, was killed. President Franklin D. Roosevelt posthumously conferred the Distinguished Service Cross upon Kelly for his sacrifice and a monument now stands at Madison, Florida., to honor him. After the war ended it was revealed that the ship which Kelly sank was not the battleship *Haruna* but was actually a Japanese cruiser named *Ashigara.* The *Haruna* was actually operating hundreds of miles away near Malaysia at the time of the sinking.

Others, such as Commander David McCampbell, returned home as heroes and lived out their lives with memories of action-packed experiences that listed them among the world's renown. Young David McCampbell moved from Alabama with his family to West Palm Beach as a child. He graduated from the US Naval Academy during the depression in 1933 and due to lack of funds was granted an honorable discharge from the Navy which could not afford to keep him. But in 1934 he was called back and commissioned. In 1936 he received an assignment aboard the *USS Portland.*

In 1937 his flying career finally got off the ground when he reported to the Pensacola Naval Air Station for flight training. A year later he was assigned to the Fighting Squadron 4 aboard the *USS Ranger-CV-4* where he served for two years before accepting duty on the *Wasp,* which was sunk by a Japanese submarine on

September 15, 1942. He became an "Ace of Aces," a top Navy pilot who won the Medal of Honor and was credited with shooting down 34 Japanese aircraft in 1944 in his Hellcat within a seven-month span of time, including nine kills within a 90-minute mission, which is believed to be the world's record. He is listed as the Navy's top ace and the fourth in standing behind three Army Air Force pilots. In a 1992 interview he stated that he tried not to think of the people who were killed but, rather, simply tried to put

Photo 42 - "Ace of Aces" Capt. David McCampbell of West Palm Beach set a record in aerial warfare history during World War II. (*Florida Archives*.)

it out of his memory.

It was then that McCampbell returned to the United States to fit out the new squadron, Air Group 15, which became known as "The Fabled Fifteen." The Fabled Fifteen saw action in Iwo Jima, Formosa, the Marianas, Palau, Philippines, Nasei and

## Jim Wiggins

Shotos, climaxing with the Battle of the Philippine Sea. He was promoted to commander in 1944 and was in charge of the entire *Eissex* air group which included bombers, fighters and torpedo planes that sank more enemy ships than any other air group in the Pacific.

The most famous action took place in the Philippine Sea in what became known as the "Mariana Turkey Shoot" when the Japanese launched their planes on June 19. McCampbell began his slaughter against a second group of 80 planes and the rest is all history. President Roosevelt presented him with the Congressional Medal of Honor on October 24. In addition he retired from the Navy in 1964 with the Navy Cross, the Silver Star Medal, the Legion of Merit and three Distinguished Flying Crosses. He died in Florida on June 30, 1996, after a lengthy illness and was buried at Arlington Cemetery.

Local communities in Florida honored their returning heroes in many different ways. Corporal James H. Mills of Fort

Photo 43 - Servicemen read the news about the Japanese surrender in the St. Petersburg Times. (*Florida Archives*)

Meade was honored in a most unusual way after being wounded while assigned to the 3rd Division in the Anzio, Italy, beachhead.

## Jim Wiggins

A recipient of the Congressional Medal of Honor, he returned to his birthplace to become a farmer. Gifts were heaped upon him by the nearby city of Bartow in the form of a tractor, plows and tools that would assist him with his physical disability. He not only farmed but also became a wildlife officer and a representative of the Veterans' Administration in Gainesville, Florida.

Photo 44 - Sailors climb the light posts in Miami to celebrate the end of war. (*Florida Archives*)

Unfortunately, Mills was beaten and run over by three men that he and his caretaker stopped on the road to help. He died on November 11, 1973, and was buried at Oak Hill Cemetery in Lakeland, Florida. The gifts that Cpl. Mills received from the citizens of Polk County are now on display in front of the courthouse in Bartow. All local communities in Florida were proud of their returning veterans but few went so far as the residents in Polk County to express their appreciation.

V-E Day arrived on May 8, 1945, when peace came to Europe. Only Japan was left. V-J Day was celebrated on August 15, 1945, after the explosion of the bombs on Hiroshima and Nagasaki. Another round of celebrations took place on September 2 when the Japanese formally surrendered. World War II was now officially over.

Most of the men who gave their lives did not do so in any spectacular manner but, rather, simply died while carrying out

Photo 45 - Headlines from Jacksonville's Florida Times-Union proclaims hope for a world of peace. (*Florida Archives*)

their duty. Some died in trenches or on battlefields with their comrades. Others went down with their ships or met their fate in exploding aircraft or while floating down in their parachutes like ducks in the sights of hunters' guns. Some died alone.

Others gave up their struggle while gasping for their last breath in a Red Cross ambulance or while attempting to recover in a clinic or hospital. Some, like Earl Hardin, returned to tell their personal story without much fanfare. Others, like Commander

## Jim Wiggins

McCampbell became renown for their outstanding performance. Each, however, was a hero in his own right. The war's end had come after a long and arduous struggle and Floridians can be particularly proud of the role, which they played so valiantly.

# Notes

## Chapter One: *The Growing Signs of War*

1. Maddox, Robert James. *The United States and World war II*, p. 81.
2. Ibid., p. 82.
3. See Jon Meacham's *Franklin and Winston, An Intimate Portrait of An Epic*
4. *Friendship* for a complete analysis of the solidarity and friendship of these two
5. Leaders.
1. Burnett, Gene. *Florida's Past*, vol. 2, p. 188.
2. Ibid.
3. Ibid, p. 189.
4. Maddox, p. 75.
5. President Franklin D. Roosevelt's fireside chat, May 26, 1940.
6. Ibid.
7. Ibid.
8. Ibid.
9. Ibid.
10. Gilbert, Martin. The Second World War, p. 41.
11. Fleming, Thomas. The New Dealers War, p. 41.
12. Florida: A Writer's Guide to the Southernmost State, 1939.
13. Mormino, Gary R., Florida Humanities Council, January 15, 1904, p. 6.

14. Tebeau, Charlton W., and Marina, William. A History of Florida, 3rd. Ed., p. 397.
15. Maddox, p. 82.
16. Fleming, pp. 1,2.
17. Ibid., p. 3.
18. Congressional Record, 77th Congress, 1st Session, 1941, 87, A5448-A5451.
19. Fleming, Ibid.

**Chapter Two:** *War Is Declared*
1. Lord, Walter. Day of Infamy, p. 208.
2. 2, Ibid., p.56.
3. Ibid., p. 3.
4. Ibid.

**Chapter Three:** *Florida's Military Bases*
1. Freitus, Joseph and Ann. Florida: The War Years 1938-1945, p. 2. Note: This book is an invaluable resource for the war years in Florida, providing detailed information, in particular, about the military establishments.
2. Ibid., p. 56.
3. Ibid. p. 3.
4. Ibid.,
5. Ibid., p. 7.
6. Ibid., p. 36.
7. FSU Report, Florida Military Bases
8. Freitus, p. 8.
9. Ibid.
10. Ibid., p. 16.
11. Tebeau, p. 404.

12. Freitus, p. 80.
13. Ibid.
14. Ibid.
15. Courtesy of U. S. Navy files.

## Chapter Four: *The War on Florida's East Coast*

1. Keegan, John, The Second World War, p. 2,
2. Gannon, Michael. Operation Drumbeat p. 76.
3. Gannon, Michael. Black May, pp. 80, 81.
4. Kahn, David, Seizing the Enigma, pp. 210-211.
5. Gannon, Black Day, p. 79.
6. Ibid., p. 81.
7. Ibid., p. 296.
8. Kleinberg, Eliot. War in Paradise, p. 29.
9. Freitus, p. 67.
10. Gannon. Drumbeat, p. 363.
11. Ibid., as quoted in Hardegen's Auf Gefechtstationen (Roreas Verlag, Leipzig, 1943), p. 134.
12. *St. Petersburg Times*, Beb. 10, 2003.
13. Ibid.
14. As reported by Gannon at the Fueher Naval Conference, March 12, 1942,
15. Doenitz KTB, Reel 3979/PG30306/a, April 15, 1942.
16. Fueher Naval Conference
17. Ibid.
18. Brit, Lora Sinks. My Gold Coast, p. 188.
19. Ibid., p.190.
20. Ibid., pp. 190, 191.

## Chapter Five: *U-boats in the Gulf*

1. The *Mobile Press Register*, June 21, 1942. Reports from survivors differ but all agreed that the encounter with their enemies was cordial.
2. Cronenberg, Allen. *Gulf Coast Historical Review*, Vol. 5, no. 2.
3. *St. Petersburg Times*. July 19, 1942.
4. The Courier, Hauma, Louisiana. February 4, 2001.
5. KTBU-506 Reel 3066/PG30566/2, June 15, 1942.
6. Dunnigan, James F. and Noff, Albert A. Dirty Little Secrets of World War 11, p. 273.

## Chapter Six: *Florida Is Invaded*

1. Derr, Mark. Some Kind of Paradise, p. 336.
2. Billinger, p. 1.
3. Ibid., 3.
4. See Billinger, Chapter 6, Escapes: The Individualists, the Threatened, and the Alienated for a comprehensive view of this subject.
5. Again, listings and detailed information on this subject are offered in Billinger's excellent review of the entire POW operation in Florida.
6. Billinger, p. 17.
7. Ibid, pp. 17, 18,

## Chapter Seven: *Florida's Economic Expansion*

1. Keegan, p. 103.
2. Freitus, p. 84.
3. Ibid., p. 85.
4. Derr, p. 330.
5. Tebeau, p. 404.

6. Ibid., p. 305.

## Chapter Eight: *The Home Front*

1. Derr, p. 336.
2. Gannon, Michael, ed. The New History of Florida, p. 128
3. See Robert Lee Rhodes' Claude Pepper, His Role in Foreign Policy.
4. Courtesy of The Florida State Archives.
5. Website available on Hit Parade.com for complete listings of songs on Saturday night radio.
6. Armbrusler, Ann. Life and Times of Miami Beach, p. 100.
7. Ibid.
8. See Barett Tillman's Hellcat Aces of World War 2 for this and other stories of
9. Airmen who fought in the war.

## Chapter Nine: *They Remember*

1. The author is indebted to Earl Hardin's wife, Jewel, for permission to use this material. This personal account is particularly unique in the fact that Earl was both a prisoner of war and also served in the Russian army. This graphic portrayal by a Floridian, though extremely harsh and unusual, is symbolic of frightening experiences shared by many in a war that was hell.
2. Earl Hardin was a younger first cousin of the author's father and lived close to the Wiggins family at Ellenton, Fla. The author recalls vividly when Earl left for duty and remembers his return to his wife at his mother's nearby home. As a teenager the author remembers becoming fascinated with all the war stories told.
3. This name should not be confused with President Theodore Roosevelt. In 1941, Teddy Roosevelt, a cousin of President Franklin D. Roosevelt, then 54 years old and a veteran of World War 1, asked to be recalled to active duty. In 1942 he was promoted to Brigadier General. He landed at Utah

## Jim Wiggins

Beach with the 4th Infantry Division in June of 1944 and died in Normandy the following month of a heart attack at age 57. He was greatly loved and respected by all the troops and was awarded the Medal of Honor posthumously for his extraordinary heroism.

4. A fictitious name was used by Earl.
5. This material was recorded from memory in the 1980s and no changes have been made to assure accuracy in geographical details, killings, etc.
6. Earl Hardin died on Nov. 3, 1992, at the age of 81.

# Bibliography

Armbrusler, Ann. *Life and Times of Miami Beach.* New York: Alfred A. Knopf, 1995.

Billinger, Robert D., Jr. *Hitler's Soldiers in the Sunshine State: German POWs in Florida.* Gainesville, Florida: University Press of Florida, 2000.

Bishop, Eleanor C. *Prints in the Sand-USCG Beach Patrol WW11.* Missoula, Montana: Historical Publishing Co.

Blair, Clay. *Hitler's U-Boat War: The Hunters.* New York: Random House, 1996.

Brown, Warren J. *Florida's Aviation History.* Largo, Florida: Florida Aero-Medical Consultants, 1980.

Burnett, Gene M. *Florida's Past,* vols.1, 2, 3. Sarasota, Florida: Pineapple Press, 1986-91.

Burns, James MacGreagor. *Roosevelt: The Lion and the Fox.* New York: Harcourt, Brace, and World, 1956.

Busch, Harald. *U-Boats at War.* New York: Ballantine Books, 1955.

Coles, David J. *Hell-by-the Sea: Florida's Camp Gordon Johnson in World War II.*

Florida Historical Quarterly 73 (July, 1994), pp. 1-22.

Cremer, Peter. *U-Boat Commander: A Periscope View of the Battle of the Atlantic.* Annapolis, Md.: Naval Institute Press, 1985,

Derr, Mark. *Some Kind of Paradise.* New York: William Morrow and Company, Inc., 1989.

Divine, Robert A. *The Invasion of Neutrality: Franklin D. Roosevelt and the Struggle over the Arms Embargo.* Chicago: University of Chicago Press, 1962.

Doenitz, Karl. *Memoirs: Ten Years and Twenty Days,* trans. R..H. Stevens with David Woodward. Cleveland, Ohio: World Publishing Co., 1959.

Dunnigan, James F. and Albert A. Noff. *Dirty Little Secrets of World War II.* New York: William Morrow and Company, Inc., 1994.

Fleming, Thomas. *The New Dealers War.* New York: Holt and Company, 2001.

Frank, Wolfgang. *The Sea Wolves: The Story of U-Boats at War.* New York: Rinehart & Company, 1955.

Freitus, Joseph and Anne. *Florida: The War Years 1938-1945.* Niceville, Florida: Wind Canyon Publishing, Inc., 1998.

Gannon, Michael. *Black May.* New York: Harper Collins, 1998.

Gannon, Michael. *Operation Drumbeat.* New York: Harper and Row Publishers, 1990.

Gannon, Michael. *The New History of Florida,* ed. (Chapter 18, *World War II* by Gary R. Mormino) Gainesville, Florida: University Press of Florida, 1996.

Gilbert, Martin. *The Second World War: A Complex History.* New York: Holt and Company, 1989.

Kahn, David. *Seizing the Enigma.* New York: Barnes and Noble Books, 1991,

Keegan, John. *The Second World War.* New York: Penguin Books, 1989.

Kleinberg, Eliot. *War in Paradise.* Melborne, Florida.: The Florida Historical Society Press, 1999.

Lord, Walter. *Day of Infamy.* New York: Henry Holt and Company, 1957.

Maddox, Robert James. *The United States and World War II.* Boulder Col.: Westview Press, 1992.

McIver, Stuart. *Glimpses of South Florida History.* Miami: Florida Flair Books, 1988.

Meacham, Jon. *Franklin and Winston, An Intimate Portrait of an Epic Friendship.*

New York: Random House, 2003.

Rhodes, Robert Lee, Jr. *Claude Pepper, His Role in Foreign Policy.* Emory University, Georgia: Department of History, 1969.

## Jim Wiggins

Sherwood, Robert E. *Roosevelt and Hopkins.* New York: Harper and Brothers, 1948.

Tebeau, Charlton and William Marina. *A History of Florida,* 3rd ed. Miami: University of Miami Press, 1999.

Tebeau, Charlton W. *Florida's Last Frontier.* Coral Gables: University of Miami Press, 1957.

Terraine, John. *The U-Boat Wars, 1916-1945.* New York: G.P. Putnam's Sons, 1989.

Tillman, Barrett. *Hellcat Aces of World War 2.* Wellingborough, UK: Osprey Publishing, 1996.

Werner, Herbert A. *Iron Coffins.* New York: Bantam Books, 1978.

Wiggins, Jim. *Glimpses of Florida's Past.* Kearney, Nebraska: Morris Publishing, 2002.

Wiggins, Melanie. *Torpedoes in the Gulf.* College Station: Texas A&M University Press, 1995.

Wynne, Lewis H., ed, *Florida at War.* Saint Leo, Florida: Saint Leo College Press, 1993.

# Index

## A

Accentuate the Positive ....... 141
Africa ................................... 118
Air Transport Command 44, 57, 118
Alachua ................................. 41
Albert Whitted Field ............. 42
Alligator Point ...................... 39
Amelia City .......................... 35
Anna Maria Island .. 43, 81, 137, 138, 142
Army Air Corps ............ 37, 146
Army bases ........................... 36
Atlantic Charter .................... 14
Aunt Myrtle ............. 19, 21, 139
Australia ....................... 27, 118
Avon Park ........... 28, 41, 42, 44

## B

Banana River ....... 34, 49, 53, 71
Bay Pines ............................. 53
Bayboro Harbor .................... 42
Beer Barrel Polka ................ 140
Big Cypress Swamp ........... 116
Black Creek .......................... 35
Black May ............. 63, 179, 184
Black Point .......................... 31
Blimp Patrol Squadron .......... 49
Blue Orchid ........................ 140
Blueberry Hill .................... 140
Boca Chica Key ................... 48
Boca Raton .. 45, 53, 74, 82, 148
Boynton Inlet ....................... 74
Brazil ........................ 3, 27, 118
Breakers Hotel .................... 148
Brownsville ......................... 53
Bunnell ................................ 35
Burma ................................ 118
Bushnell ................. 53, 59, 112
Bushnell-Lyons ............ 59, 112

## C

Camp Blanding. vii, viii, 31, 32, 33, 53, 101, 102, 105, 122
Camp Foster ........................ 31
Camp Gordon Johnson .. vii, 38, 183
Canada ....................... 6, 26, 27
Cannon Ball Express ........... 118
Cape of Good Hope .............. 83
Care Packages .................... 138
Carrabelle, Fl ....................... 39
Catfish Point ........................ 42
Cecil Field .................... 35, 53
Cedar Key ............................ 41
Chafe .................................. 35
China ............... 27, 47, 118, 139
Civil War ....... 12, 36, 48, 84, 95
Civilian Pilot Training program ................................ 41, 44
Cocoa Beach ........................ 34
Committee on Foreign Relations ...................... 120
Congressional Medal of Honor ............................ 173, 174
Coral Gables ................. 53, 185
Correy Field ........................ 36
Corsair Navy ....................... 70
Crescent City ....................... 53
Cronenberg, Allen ............... 180
Czechoslovakia ............. 27, 167

## D

Dale Mabry Army Air Field..38
Daytona Beach ................35, 53
DDT ......................................116
Deep in the Heart of Texas..140
Defender..............................87
Deland..................................54
Democrats ...........................15
Development of Landings
    Areas .............................29
DeWayne............... 19, 139, 169
Dinner Key......................47, 54
Distinguished Flying Cross.173
Doenitz, Karl ......................183
Donald Duck Navy..............117
Dr. Pepper sodas ..................13
Drumbeaters ........................66
Dunedin.........................54, 111
Dyers Point.........................114

## E

East Africa ...........................47
Eastern Airlines...................118
Eglin Army Air Field ............37
Eissex air group...................173
Ellenton, Fl...............ix, xiii, 181
Embry-Riddle School.............28

## F

Fabled Fifteen .....................172
FBI 98, 101
Ferry Command ...................45
Flagler Beach .......................54
Florida Bay....................48, 145
Florida Citrus Commission.116
Florida Defense Council .....117
Florida National Guard ..vii, 31, 121
Florida Portland Cement
    Company ....................112
Florida Southern College.....139
Florida State Guard .............122
Florida State Road Department
    ......................................110
Fools Rush In .....................140
Fort Lauderdale ... vii, 3, 54, 74, 82, 117
Fort McRee...........................36
Fort Myers ...........50, 51, 52, 54
Fort Pickens..........................36
Fort Pierce ....34, 35, 41, 55, 67, 74, 82
Fort William ........................55
France...2, 6, 26, 27, 33, 65, 66, 96, 120, 159
Ft. Lauderdale..................xi, 46
Fullers Earth Plant...............113
Furious.................................78

## G

Gainesville......41, 55, 174, 183, 184
Gannon, Michael.179, 181, 184
German High Command .......63
German-American Bund .......98
Gibbs Shipyards ..................113
Gilbert, Martin.............177, 184
G-Men .................................85
Great American Turkey Shoot
    .......................................65
Great Depression ...... xiii, 2, 16, 125, 140
Greece .................................27
Green Cove Springs.........35, 55
Greenville Aviation .........27, 28
Gulf of Mexico. viii, 62, 69, 81, 82, 83, 88, 90, 91, 93, 137

## H

Havana Naval Station............86
Hendricks Army Air Field.....41

Hialeah ..................................... 55
Hiroshima ............................ 175
Hit Parade ................... 140, 181
Hobe Sound .................... viii, 55
Hollywood Beach Hotel 55, 148
Holmes Beach ....................... 22
Holquist ................................ 44
Home Demonstration Office 138
Homestead ................. 45, 47, 55
Humble Oil Company ......... 116

*I*

I Left My Heart at the Stage
    Door Canteen ................ 141
Iceland .................................... 9
India ................... 27, 47, 78, 118
Italy ............................ 1, 23, 173

*J*

J.A. Jones Company ............ 114
Jacksonville .. viii, ix, 12, 30, 31,
    35, 55, 69, 71, 72, 73, 79,
    82, 96, 99, 113, 114, 117,
    120
Japan 1, 15, 20, 22, 52, 139, 175
Java Arrow, the sinking of .... 74
Jingle, Jingle, Jingle ............ 140
Joseph M. Cudahy, the sinking
    of ..................................... 84
Jupiter ........... vii, 56, 68, 74, 82
Jupiter Island ........................ 74

*K*

Kahn, David ................ 179, 184
Karachi, India ...................... 118
Kearny, the sinking of ............. 9
Keegan, John ............... 179, 184
Key West 30, 48, 49, 56, 71, 82,
    117, 119
Kleinberg, Eliot ........... 179, 184
Kline ................. 21, 81, 137, 139

Korsholm, the sinking of ....... 74

*L*

La Paz, the sinking of ........... 74
Lake Butler ........................... 41
Lake City ........................ 41, 56
Lakeland ...... 27, 28, 41, 43, 174
Lantana Field ........................ 51
Lauderdale Beach Hotel ........ 54
Lee Field ............................... 35
Legion of Merit ................... 173
Lubrafol, the sinking of ......... 74
Lynn Haven .......................... 56

*M*

Manatee River ....... 24, 113, 169
Marathon ........................ 49, 56
Mariana ............................... 173
Mariana Turkey Shoot ......... 173
Marineland ..................... 12, 58
Maxwell Field .. 36, 38, 84, 101,
    171
Maxwell Field, Alabama ....... 38
Maybe ................................. 140
Mayport ............. 34, 56, 73, 114
Melbourne .......... 41, 56, 67, 74
Merchant Marine Act .......... 111
*Mexico* ................... 6, 82, 83, 86
Miami .... vii, viii, ix, 12, 28, 44,
    47, 48, 49, 53, 55, 57, 69,
    71, 82, 83, 102, 103, 110,
    114, 117, 118, 119, 146,
    147, 181, 183, 184, 185
Miami Beach .. vii, 57, 102, 103,
    119, 146, 147, 181, 183
Miami Municipal Airport 44, 48
Miami Shipbuilding
    Corporation .................. 110
Miami Springs ...................... 57
Milkcows ............................. 68
Mill Cove ............................. 35

Milton..............................ix, 57
Mississippi River.............90, 91
Mobile Bay...........................36
Morgan City ........................57
Mormino, Gary....................177
Morrison Air Base.................30
Mosquito Fleet ..............70, 117
Motorcycle Corps................145
Mullet Key ...........................43
Munger T. Ball, the sinking of
........................................84
My Gold Coast..............77, 179

*N*

Nagasaki..............................175
Naval Air Station (NAS) vii, 31,
 34, 35, 41, 46, 49, 53, 54,
 55, 56, 57, 58, 59, 71, 115,
 171
Naval Amphibious Training
 Base..............35, 41, 55, 58
Navy Flight Surgeons............36
Nazis .............................64, 106
Netherlands ...................45, 118
Neutrality Act..vii, 4, 26, 27, 29
New Caledonia......................19
New Deal .. 14, 15, 16, 177, 184
New Orleans. 83, 84, 85, 86, 88,
 89, 115
New Smyrna Beach...............36
Niceville, Fl........................184
Normandy ..............35, 113, 182
North Africa .........................33
North Atlantic Coastal Frontier
........................................69
Norway................................27

*O*

Ocean Venus, the sinking of .74
Oh, Johnny, Oh Johnny, Oh 140

Opa Locka (Naval Reserve) .48,
 57
Operation Drumbeat .63, 66, 67,
 79, 179, 184
Orion, the German freighter
 sunk ..................................3
Orlando.......27, 41, 44, 57, 105,
 110, 119
Orlando Aero School............27
Over the Rainbow...............140

*P*

Page Field............................52
Palm Beach...30, 44, 57, 68, 79,
 118, 145, 148
Palm Beach Post...................68
Palmetto...............127, 130, 154
Pan American Airlines ........118
Pan Massachusetts, the sinking
 of ............................67, 146
Panama City ....36, 58, 110, 114
Paukenschlag.............63, 66, 67
Pearl Harbor vii, xiv, 15, 16, 19,
 20, 21, 22, 23, 26, 29, 61,
 62, 66, 81, 112, 121, 130,
 137, 140, 145
Pensacola vii, 30, 36, 37, 38, 58,
 84, 110, 115, 116, 117,
 119, 171
Pensacola Navy Yard ..........115
Pensacola Shipyard..............110
Perdido Bay, seaplane air base
........................................36
Philippines......21, 118, 139, 172
Pine Castle............................44
Pioneer..................................87
Plant City High School........137
Plow Under...........................16
Poland.2, 26, 27, 158, 161, 163,
 167
Ponce de Leon Hotel ...119, 148

Ponte Vedra Beach...96, 98, 99, 100
Port Everglades 3, 4, 46, 54, 58, 74
Praise the Lord and Pass the Ammunition ................. 141
Press Register (Mobile). 84, 180
Prussian deer hunters ............. 65
PT boats .... 34, 47, 85, 113, 116
Punta Gorda ..................... 50, 52

## R

RAF – Royal Air Force .......... 44
RAF – Royal Air Force ... vii, 27
Rainbow Report .................... 15
Ration books ....................... 129
Red Cross 6, 125, 138, 154, 160, 175
Redoubt ................................ 36
Replacement Training Center, Miami ............................ 47
Republicans .......................... 15
Reuben James, the sinking of .. 9
Ribault Bay in Mayport ......... 33
Richmond ................. 49, 58, 71
Robert E. Lee, the sinking of 12, 89, 90
Rocky Bluff ........................ 113
Rollins College flight training school ....................... 41, 44
Roosevelt and Hopkins ... 4, 185
Rosie the Riveter ................. 110
Rum and Coca Cola ............ 147
Russian army ...... 162, 163, 165, 166, 168, 181

## S

Saint Augustine ..................... 58
Saint Petersburg .................... 58
San Julian ............................. 49
Sanford ................................ 58
Santa Rosa Island ................. 36
Sarasota ..... 50, 51, 52, 169, 183
Sarasota-Manatee County Municipal Airport ........... 50
Scarecrow Patrol ................... 51
See - High Frequency Directions Findings ........ 92
See - Naval Air Station ... vii, xi, 31, 35, 36, 47, 48, 49, 53, 57
See - Strategic Air Command ........................................ 138
See - Tampa Shipbuilding .. 110, 111, 112
See Development of Landings Areas ............................ 29
Sherwood, Robert ............... 185
Silver Star Medal ................ 173
Skyway Bridge ................... 127
Sniff Kit ............... viii, 143, 144
South Africa ......................... 27
South America .... 2, 4, 6, 28, 47, 62
South Venice ........................ 43
Spruce Creek ........................ 36
SS Cycops, the sinking of ...... 64
SS Gulfamerica, the sinking of ........................................ 71
SS Ohioan, the sinking of ...... 78
St. Johns River .. 31, 33, 35, 110, 113
St. Petersburg Times .. ix, xi, 72, 86, 179, 180
State Fair ............................ 141
Straits of Florida ........ 82, 83, 91
Strategic Air Command ...... 137, 138
Stratmeyer Towers Conference ........................................ 30
Swinging on a Star ............. 141

## T

Tallahassee ........ vii, viii, 38, 59
Tampa Shipbuilding ..... 59, 110, 111
Tampico ................................. 83
Tarpon Springs ....................... 59
Tebeau, Historian Charlton W.
 ............................ 178, 185
Terra Ceia ............................. 43
The Hut Sut Song ................ 140
The White Cliffs of Dover .. 140
The Woodpecker Song ........ 140
Three Little Fishes ............... 140
Trinidad ........................ 89, 118
Trumbo Point seaplane base .. 48
Tuskeegee Airmen ................. 38
Tyndall Army Air Field ........ 37

## U

U-boats . 5, 9, 31, 35, 42, 61, 62, 63, 64, 65, 66, 67, 68, 69, 71, 76, 82, 83, 84, 85, 86, 88, 89, 91, 96, 112, 120, 180
University of Florida .... 55, 116, 135, 139
USS Capps ........................... 84

## V

Valpariso ............................. 37

Venture ............................... 87
Vera Cruz ............................ 83
Vero Beach ................... 34, 59
Versagi fleet ....................... 87

## W

W.D. Anderson, the sinking of
 ........................................ 67
WACS ........................... 43, 45
Wainwright Shipyard (Panama City) .................... 110, 114
Wakula ............................... 59
WAVES .................. 34, 41, 48
West Palm Beach . ix, 44, 47, 51, 57, 70, 74, 118, 171
White Christmas ................ 137
William C. McTarnahan ........ 86
Winter Park .................. 28, 44
World War 1 .......... xi, 180, 181
WPA ................... 12, 32, 42, 50

## Y

Ybor Channel ..................... 112
Yucatan Channel ................. 91

## Z

Zephryhills .......................... 43
Zip Your Lips .................... 133

## About the Author

JIM WIGGINS is a fourth-generation Floridian who was born in Ellenton. He is a graduate of Florida Southern College and holds an MTh Degree from the Southern California School of Theology. His books include *Glimpses of Florida's Past* and *More Glimpses of Florida's Past*, compilations of columns written for *The Observer* in Royal Palm Beach over six years. He is also the author of *Ellenton: Its Earlier Years and Troubled Waters*. His most recent book is *Manatee County*, part of the *Images in America* series. In addition, he is a contributor to numerous magazines, including *Florida Wildlife*, *Tide*, *Florida Gardening*, *Nature Photographer*, *New Directions for Better Living*, *Butterfly Gardener*, *Birds and Blooms*, and others. He and his wife currently live in The Acreage in Palm Beach County.

www.ingramcontent.com/pod-product-compliance
Lightning Source LLC
Chambersburg PA
CBHW072127160426
43197CB00012B/2020